A WOMAN'S JOURNEY TOWARD HOLINESS

Crossway books by Sheila Cragg

A Woman's Walk with God:
A Daily Guide for Prayer & Spiritual Growth

A Woman's Journey Toward Holiness:
A Daily Guide for Prayer & Godly Living

A Woman's Journey Toward Holiness

A Daily Guide for Prayer and Godly Living

Sheila Cragg

CROSSWAY BOOKS • WHEATON, ILLINOIS
A DIVISION OF GOOD NEWS PUBLISHERS

A Woman's Journey Toward Holiness

Copyright © 1997 by Sheila Cragg

Published by Crossway Books
    a division of Good News Publishers
    1300 Crescent Street
    Wheaton, Illinois 60187

Editor: Lila Bishop

Cover design and illustration: Cindy Kiple

First printing 1997

Printed in the United States of America

Most Scripture in the prayers in this book is paraphrased from the versions listed below. Scripture quoted directly is handled as follows:

Library of Congress Cataloging-in-Publication Data
Cragg, Sheila, 1938–
    A woman's journey toward holiness : a daily guide for prayer and godly living / Sheila Cragg.
        p.   cm.
    Includes bibliographical references.
    1. Women—Prayer-books and devotions—English. 2. Devotional calendars. 3. Holiness—Prayer-books and devotions—English.
4. Cragg, Sheila, 1938- . I. Title.
BV4844.C69 1997   242'.643—dc21   97-8087
ISBN 0-89107-960-2

05		04		03		02		01		00		99		98		97
15	14	13	12	11	10	9	8	7	6	5	4	3	2	1

CONTENTS

ACKNOWLEDGMENTS

A sincere thank you to friends and family who made this book possible by their prayers and encouragement. God, in His gracious wisdom and in divinely appointed and surprising ways, sent the assistance and materials I needed.

As always, my love and appreciation go to my husband, Ron, who rises early every morning and holds me up in prayer. He has sacrificed a great deal and supported me through this entire process.

Pastor Bruce McClain edited and carefully checked the manuscript for theological clarity, loaned me his books, sermon notes, and other valuable materials. He was kindly available to discuss the content of this book and was a constant source of information and encouragement, for which I am deeply grateful.

Judie Frank has been my friend, listening heart, and faithful prayer partner throughout this journey. Her own ministry through her poetry has blessed me. The Lord gave my friend Nancy Hopkins the idea for this book. She, too, has been my dear friend and prayer supporter. Shirlee Hickey, friend and walking partner, has been sensitive to the Holy Spirit's prompting and loaned me many books and other materials that proved to be exactly what I needed at the perfect time.

I am thankful for the women at Pine Grove Baptist Church who attended my class on leading a holy life. The personal notes they sent me, their friendship, prayers, and transparency constantly ministered to me.

The staff at Crossway Books were a joy and blessing to work with, especially Leonard Goss and Lila Bishop. Lila was gracious and supportive throughout the writing process. She loaned me her books, made many helpful suggestions, and gave her usual excellent editorial touch to the manuscript.

INTRODUCTION

*T*he idea for this book came in an unusual way. As I was praying about what to write, I asked my friend Nancy Hopkins, "Do you have any suggestions for devotional books that you'd want to read?"

"I don't have any ideas, but I'm sure God has something." Nancy paused, and then said, "Surrendering to God's ways."

"What do you mean?" I asked.

"It seems that all I'm hearing from women I've been talking to lately has to do with their struggles with submission. They're fighting against it. Submitting to what the Lord desires is difficult for me, too, especially since my husband is out of work. I've had to lay myself and everything I am before the Lord. I prayed, 'Let it be done to me as You will, Lord.' I'm continually brought back to the same place of surrendering my anxieties, fears, and needs."

I realized that I struggled with the same conflicts of trying to surrender my needs and concerns to the Lord while at the same time wanting Him to do things my way.

When Nancy speaks, I listen. I've learned that God gives her insights beyond even her understanding. And so I included her suggestion along with five ideas for devotionals to Crossway Books.

To my surprise, I was asked to write the book about surrendering to God's ways and leading a holy life, though I had only sent two sentences on the subject for the proposal. I realized that it made the most sense to write that book, because it built on the theme of deepening your devotional life in my previous book, *A Woman's Walk with God.*

I quickly learned, however, that I was presumptuous in thinking I could write a book about holiness. I hadn't realized how little I knew about surrendering to God's ways and practicing holy living.

The deeper I got into the book, the more I was challenged, chastised, and convicted in my own personal and spiritual life. As I worked on every chapter of this book, my willingness to be obedient and submit to the Lord was tested. The validity of my faith, commitment, and love for the Lord were being tried in the very areas I was writing about.

The pressure to apply personally what God was teaching me was unrelenting. I felt as if He were putting me through a rigorous training program, and I wanted to quit the spiritual race more than once.

In fact, I lost it! I hit a wall, stumbled, and injured myself. I was flattened. We were struck by a series of intense trials, and I could hardly write a word for four weeks as I neared completion of this book. I wondered if I could get up and finish the race.

I was reminded of many Christians who have quit the race. Many dropped out because the pressure and the pain were more than they were willing to endure. Injuries caused by sin have knocked others out of the race.

I had a choice. I could quit, or I could continue to deal with my sins, which were a lack of discipline in several areas of my life. I could endure the pain of the trials we were experiencing, resist the urge to drop out, release my hurts to the Lord, and finish the task.

I realized that I needed to submit myself to the Lord's discipline and keep on running the race, even though I felt I wasn't making much progress in becoming holy. Though I've been a Christian for forty-two years and have completed this book, I feel as if I'm only beginning to understand what it means to be a genuinely godly person. It has been a most humbling experience.

As God has sifted and refined my life, I've shared my own struggles and discoveries that have helped me on my own journey toward holiness, and I pray these will be of some help to all who read this book.

The women in the class I taught on holiness expressed their own conflicting feelings about what it means to be a godly person. We may desire to be holy, but we realize how much we fall short of submitting to God's ways so we can become the person God desires us to be. Holiness seems too great for us, too awesome and awful.

Holiness and the accountability of surrender to God seem so remote from the realities of everyday living. We may desire to be holy, and yet we run from convictions that call us to make godly choices. We flee because of our pride and our tremendous fear of the requirements of holiness.

We need to realize that becoming a godly person is a process and that we will never become completely holy in our lifetime. We all need a beginning place where we can grow in godliness. So pack away the guilt and "shoulds" and feelings of inferiority and unworthiness. Start where you are, and begin this journey with an open heart and willing spirit to become the godly person the Lord desires you to be.

Here are some suggestions to help you use this devotional book. *A Woman's Journey Toward Holiness* can be used by individuals or small groups. The devotionals don't have to be completed in a week, so give yourself the freedom to work through the book at your own pace.

Each week's opening page has a Scripture passage that can be memorized. Plan to read the chapter the first day and complete the Day One devotional. Before you start reading each day's devotional, write the date on the blank line at the top of the page.

Later you may want to reread what you've written. The dates will help you relate that time to the events and concerns you were experiencing during that period. You will be able to compare where you were in your spiritual life and how you have progressed since then.

Each day's devotion begins with Scripture passages to read that correlate with the theme of the chapter. The "Scripture Reading" and "Practicing the Spiritual Life" were based on the *Holy Bible: New International Version* (NIV). Using this Bible or another modern-day version will make it easier to answer the questions in that section. You may also enjoy looking up passages in several different versions to gain a greater depth of meaning.

Under "Practicing the Spiritual Life," the first set of questions pertain to the "Scripture Reading," and the second set are for personal application. Take time to seriously consider those questions, to pray, and to seek the Lord's direction for your own spiritual life. The questions are meant to help you grow in godliness and to apply the truths of Scripture to your life.

Feel free to make notes in this book. Lined spaces are included for you to write answers, personal thoughts, and spiritual insights.

A personalized Scripture prayer follows "Practicing the Spiritual Life." The prayers can help you present your requests to the Lord, confess sin, and praise and worship Him using Scripture as a means of intercession. (I used the pronouns *I*, *me*, and *my*, and put the verses in my own words.) Then you may use these Scriptures from various Bible versions as prayers. And finally there are more spaces for you to record "Praises, Prayers, and Personal Notes."

A Woman's Journey Toward Holiness concludes with a retreat for spiritual renewal, for which I include "Plans for a Small Group Study and Spiritual Retreat." It is my prayer that those who use this book may know the joy of having a desire for holiness, a spiritually renewed life, and a greater love for our magnificent Savior and Lord. "Since we have these promises, dear friends, let us purify ourselves from everything that contaminates body and spirit, perfecting holiness out of reverence for God" (2 Cor. 7:1).

WEEK ONE

Respond to Christ's Call to Be Holy

"But just as he who called you is holy,
so be holy in all you do;
for it is written:
'Be holy, because I am holy.'"

1 PETER 1:15-16

*T*he fruit orchards and gardens had an untamed beauty about them. Orange nasturtiums and fluorescent blue morning glories carelessly wandered wherever they pleased. Native flowers, vines, and wheat-colored weeds grew in wild profusion around the conference center buildings, church, and an old mansion.

The center had once been the estate of a wealthy family. They had built the mansion of local Santa Barbara stone in the early part of the century. The rooms were grand, enormous, and decorated with exquisite antiques. Now the mansion was used for individuals who desired to have a private retreat. It was a quiet place to rest, read, and pray.

The Locked Door

Late Thursday when I arrived at the center, I was graciously met at the front door of the mansion by a hostess. The double doors were dark, immense, and ornate.

She handed me a key and said, "You'll need to carry your key whenever you leave. The doors are locked to keep those who are attending other conferences from entering the house. But don't turn the antique door handle; it's broken and can't be replaced. Just turn the key and push on the door."

After thanking her I went to my room, forgetting about her instructions. Friday morning I walked the grounds, read my spiritual retreat book, and journaled. When I tried to reenter the house, however, I had difficulty unlocking the door. I tried to turn the door handle and then quickly remembered that I shouldn't touch it.

"Lord, help me," I prayed in exasperation.

I turned the key again and pushed the door, and it swung open.

An ordinary experience, such as trying to unlock a door, may be the means by which the Lord makes Himself known to us. "These doors remind me of the painting of Jesus knocking at the door, seeking entry into our lives," I wrote in my journal.

"'Here I am! I stand at the door and knock. If anyone hears my voice and opens the door, I will come in and eat with him, and he with me'" (Rev. 3:20). Jesus is knocking, calling to us, and waiting for us to open the door to a more holy life.

At first we may not hear Jesus calling us or recognize that it is He who is knocking. We may hear a sound, but we don't know where it's coming from. We search the house or check the door and then dismiss the idea that we heard anything at all.

If we are willing to listen, we may recognize when Jesus knocks. He is waiting for us to open the door and ask, "Lord, help me be the godly person you desire me to be."

Once we open that door, we realize that Jesus has been speaking to us through His Word or a persistent spiritual yearning. He is making us aware of our need for deep personal communion with Him. He is awakening us to our need to become more like Him and our need to have a deeper devotional life.

Unlocking the Door

By Friday afternoon, I still couldn't unlock the door. I asked a man who was about to enter the house to show me.

"It's simple," he said.

Attempting to lead a holy life is similar to a lock that is stuck or hard to turn. What is so simple for others to unlock may be difficult for us. They may easily enter into a committed Christian life without hesitation, while those same doors seem shut to us. We may struggle with a stubborn lock—a sin, a habit, an attitude that we need to overcome. Then someone simply demonstrates how the key works in the lock, but we still don't understand how to open the door ourselves. We can't seem to free ourselves from sins that lock us out.

Though the man showed me how to unlock the door, I had not tried it myself. Friday at dinner again I couldn't open the door. I knocked, but no one heard me. I began to feel panicky and fearful that I wouldn't get in. I ran around the mansion to a door with windows. I was thankful when someone heard me knocking and let me in.

We may also knock at Jesus' door and seek entry into His presence. "'Ask and it will be given you; seek and you will find; knock and the door will be opened'" (Matt. 7:7).

What are you to ask Jesus for? Ask for the desire to be holy; seek after a fruitful, Spirit-filled life. Knock until the door of your heart opens to the Lord. Let Him come in and transform your life.

Turning the Key

Saturday morning the door lock stymied me again. When I tried the key, I listened for the click and pushed the door; it wouldn't budge. I was exasperated and humiliated.

Then I remembered one woman's casual remark. "If you don't catch it the first time, you have to turn the key all the way around a second time."

I turned the key around again, and the door opened.

"I have finally conquered the lock on the front door of the stone house," I wrote in my journal Saturday evening.

To lead a holy life, we need to keep on turning the key, keep on listening for the click until the key catches, and keep on pushing the door until it opens. How many times do we unlock doors in our lifetime? We must repeat the process of seeking to lead a holy life time and time again.

The Fear of Holiness

If only we could conquer this life of holiness with fewer fears and frustrations, but then it is not we who must conquer. We cannot unlock the door alone. We cannot overcome sin by ourselves. Consider these questions: Are we willing to open the door to Jesus and surrender ourselves entirely to Him? Are we willing to be holy, or have we shut the door because of our pride and fear of what He'll ask of us?

"We tend to have mixed feelings about the holy. There is a sense in which we are at the same time attracted to it and repulsed by it. Something draws us toward it, while at the same time we want to run away from it."[1]

I have mixed feelings about being godly because I know myself. I'm quick to sin and slow to be holy. All it takes is a few unguarded words, a deliberate or impulsive wrongful action, and a sinful thought, which come so naturally. Holiness is supernatural and requires that we submit ourselves to God's Word and to the Holy Spirit so that He may transform us. Godliness is a whole new way of being.

I war with conflicting feelings about leading a holy life. I desire to be holy, and yet I run from convictions that call me to make godly choices. I flee because of my pride, my continual battle with sin, and my apprehension about the requirements of holiness. I fear God, but not always in the way He desires.

"We fear God because He is holy. Our fear is not the fear of the Lord the Bible enjoins. It is a servile fear, a fear born of dread. God is too great for us; He is too awesome. He makes difficult demands on us. He is the Mysterious Stranger who threatens our security. In His presence we quake and tremble. Meeting Him personally may be our greatest trauma."[2]

Knowing God and becoming holy is traumatic, because it calls us to make changes in our character, conduct, and thought life but not in the legalistic way we often envision. We may think that holy people are sour, stern, and strict, that they live by a severe set of rules. We may believe that being holy is adhering to a long list of prohibitions. We must follow certain do's and don'ts about how we dress, what we do, whom we associate with, and where we go.[3] When I was a young Christian, the big sins were dancing, drinking, smoking, going to movies, and playing cards. What a contrast to the list of serious sins today!

Called to Be Holy

If we're going to respond to God's call to be holy, we need to realize that holiness encompasses far more than a list of don'ts. We need to understand the true meaning of holiness, which God defines for us in the first commandment: "You shall have no other gods before me" (Ex. 20:3).

> The duties required in the first commandment are knowing and acknowledging God to be the only true God and our God; and to worship and glorify him accordingly by thinking, meditating, remembering, highly esteeming, honoring, adoring, choosing, loving, desiring, fearing him; believing him; trusting, hoping, delighting, rejoicing in him; being zealous for him; calling upon him, giving all praise and thanks, and yielding all obedience and submission to him with the whole person; being careful in all things to please him, and sorrowful when in any thing he is offended; and walking humbly with him.[4]

What a glorious description of what it means to lead a holy life. If we put no other gods first in our lives, we'd be transformed. If we were sorrowful when in anything we offended God, we wouldn't be as concerned about "petty" prohibitions as we are about dishonoring Him in anything we do and say. If we yielded ourselves in all obedience and loving submission to our sovereign Lord with all our heart and all our soul and all our strength, we'd honor Him (Deut. 6:5). If we adored, esteemed, and worshiped the great I AM in all His magnificent holiness, we'd walk humbly in His presence.

Bearing God's Likeness

If we're going to be holy, we need to become more like Christ.

When our grandson Byron was born, we asked the question that families often debate: "Whom does he look like?"

"He looks just like his father," one grandparent said.

I said, "I think he looks like his Grandpa Bruce."

Usually it's difficult to tell whose likeness a newborn bears, but we delight in trying to decide anyway.

Our heavenly Father Himself seemed to take delight in finding His likeness in His children, for He created us in His image in the first place (Gen. 1:26-27). Moreover, He predetermined that we were to be conformed to the likeness of His Son (Rom. 8:29). "Long ago even before he made the world, God loved us and chose us in Christ to be holy and without fault in his eyes. His unchanging plan has always been to adopt us into his own family by bringing us to himself through Jesus Christ. And this gave him great pleasure" (Eph. 1:4-5 NLT).

How joyous it is that God finds great pleasure in adopting us into His family. What an honor that He created us in His image. What a privilege to bear His likeness.

As our grandson grew older, he resembled both sides of the family, but he looks more like his father than anyone else. In a similar way, we're to grow into our heavenly Father's likeness. We're to change from spiritual infants to mature Christians.

So just what does our heavenly Father "look" like? "But just as he who called you is holy, so be holy in all you do; for it is written: 'Be holy, because I am holy'" (1 Peter 1:15-16).

Our first thought may be that becoming holy and bearing God's likeness is impossible. Our loving Father, however, knows we're imperfect and that becoming holy is a maturing process. "God does not require a perfect, sinless life to have fellowship with Him, but He does require that we be serious about holiness, that we grieve over sin in our lives instead of justifying it, and that we earnestly pursue holiness as a way of life."[5]

Yes, becoming holy would be impossible if it were entirely up to us. But the good news is that making people holy is the work of the Holy Spirit. We need only to yield to this process and cooperate with the Holy One who lives within us. Through Scripture and the Holy Spirit's power, we're assured that God *will give us everything* we need to grow in faith and godliness. "His divine power has given us everything we need for life and godliness through our knowledge of him who called us by his own glory and goodness" (2 Peter 1:3).

Holy Humility

My inability to learn something as simple as unlocking a door was humbling. I wondered what God was trying to teach me through such a confounding experience. I came to realize that holiness humbles us and opens our eyes to our true condition before God. We see the impossibility of becoming holy by our own strength and recognize our weaknesses. As we humbly rely on the Lord to change us, we experience the transforming work of the Holy Spirit in our lives.

At the same time, we need to realize the frailty of our human condition; we will not attain absolute spiritual perfection in this life. But we may look forward to that day when we'll be pure and holy as that heavenly door opens and we pass from this earth into our Lord's presence. "The communion in glory with Christ, which the members of the invisible church enjoy immediately after death, is in that their souls are then made perfect in holiness and received into the highest heavens, where they behold the face of God in light and glory. . . . "[6]

Scripture Reading: Exodus 20:3; Leviticus 20:7-8, 26

Practicing the Spiritual Life
Why did God call us to be holy? What do we need to do to become godly?

_____

_____

_____

Pray and ask the Lord to show you in what ways He desires you to consecrate yourself to Him. Then write a note of commitment and dedication to Him.

_____

_____

_____

Prayer
"Among the gods there is none like you, O Lord; no deeds can compare with yours." For Lord my God, You are God of gods and Lord of lords, You are the great God, mighty and awesome. You are the Lord my God; I will consecrate myself to You and be holy, because You are holy. I will remember to obey all Your commands and will be consecrated to You. My heart shall rejoice in You, because I have trusted in Your holy name. (Ps. 86:8 not paraphrased; Deut. 10:17a; Lev. 11:44a; Num. 15:40; Ps. 33:21 KJV paraphrased)

Prayers, Praises, and Personal Notes

_____

_____

_____

_____

_____

Scripture Reading: Genesis 1:26-27; Romans 8:29

Practicing the Spiritual Life

How did God create us and for what purpose?

_____

_____

_____

In what ways do you need to become more conformed to Jesus' likeness?

_____

_____

_____

Prayer

Father, the first man is of the earth, earthy: the second man is You, Lord, from heaven. And as I have borne the image of the earthy, I shall also bear Your heavenly image. And may I, with open face behold as in a glass Your glory, Lord, and be changed into Your same image from glory to glory; for this comes from You, Lord, the Spirit. Take this weak mortal body of mine and change it into a glorious body like Your own, using the same mighty power that You will use to conquer everything, everywhere. (1 Cor. 15:47, 49 KJV; 2 Cor. 3:18 KJV, RSV; Phil. 3:21 NLT paraphrased)

Prayers, Praises, and Personal Notes

_____

_____

_____

_____

_____

Scripture Reading: 2 Peter 1:2-11

Practicing the Spiritual Life

God calls us to be holy. What qualities do we need to add to our lives in ever-increasing measure so that we may become godly?

_____

_____

_____

What specific quality will you make every effort to begin adding to your life this week?

_____

_____

_____

Prayer

O God, You have called me to be holy. You made me holy by means of Christ Jesus, just as You did all Christians everywhere—whoever calls upon Your name, Jesus Christ, my Lord and theirs. I believe this and will keep myself pure, just as You are pure, Lord. I will love what is good, be self-controlled, upright, holy and disciplined. I will pursue righteousness, godliness, faith, love, endurance, and gentleness. (1 Cor. 1:2b NLT; 1 John 3:3 NLT; Titus 1:8; 1 Tim. 6:11b paraphrased)

Prayers, Praises, and Personal Notes

_____

_____

_____

_____

_____

Scripture Reading: Psalm 24:3-6

Practicing the Spiritual Life
What does a person receive who has clean hands and a pure heart?

_____

_____

_____

What sins do you need cleansing from so that you may have clean hands and a pure heart?

_____

_____

_____

Prayer
Hear, O Holy Lord, when I cry with my voice. Have mercy upon me, answer me, and help me. When You said, "Seek My face," my heart said to You, "Your face, Lord, will I seek." And I will purify myself from everything that contaminates my body and spirit, perfecting holiness out of reverence for You. I will flee evil desires and pursue righteousness, faith, love, and peace, along with those who call on You, Lord, out of a pure heart. I glory in Your holy name; I seek You and my heart rejoices. I seek You, Lord, and Your strength; I will seek Your face forevermore. (Ps. 27:7-8 KJV; 2 Cor. 7:1; 2 Tim. 2:22; Ps. 105:3-4 paraphrased)

Prayers, Praises, and Personal Notes

_____

_____

_____

_____

Scripture Reading: 1 Thessalonians 4:1-8

Practicing the Spiritual Life

What is God's will for us? What must we abstain from in order to lead a holy life?

_____

_____

_____

Write the steps you will take to overcome a certain sin in your life this week.

_____

_____

_____

Prayer

God of grace and mercy, cleanse me from all my impurities and from all my idols. Sanctify me through and through, separate me from profane things, make me pure and wholly consecrated to You; and may my spirit and soul and body be preserved sound and complete and found blameless at Your coming, Lord Jesus Christ. For faithful are You who call me to Yourself, and utterly trustworthy, and You will also fulfill Your call by hallowing and keeping me. (Ezek. 36:25b; 1 Thess. 5:23-24 AMP paraphrased)

Prayers, Praises, and Personal Notes

_____

_____

_____

_____

_____

Scripture Reading: Ephesians 1:3-6

Practicing the Spiritual Life
What did God bless us with, choose us for, and predestine us to be?

_____

_____

_____

Write a psalm of praise for the blessing of being adopted into God's family.

_____

_____

_____

Prayer
I will stand up and bless You, O Lord my God, forever and ever: blessed be Your glorious name, which is exalted above all blessing and praise. Father God, strengthen and confirm and establish my heart faultlessly pure and unblameable in holiness in Your sight, at the coming of my Lord Jesus Christ, the Messiah, with all His saints, the holy and glorified people of God! Amen, so be it! (Neh. 9:5b KJV; 1 Thess. 3:13 AMP paraphrased)

Prayers, Praises, and Personal Notes

_____

_____

_____

_____

_____

_____

Scripture Reading: Revelation 4

Practicing the Spiritual Life
How is God worshiped and glorified in heaven?

_____

_____

_____

Express honor and glory to God for His holiness and tell what the hope of heaven means to you.

_____

_____

_____

Prayer
Glorious God of heaven, You are in Your holy temple; You are on Your heavenly throne. Who is like You, the One who sits enthroned on high, who stoops down to look on the heavens and the earth? Living Lord, I exalt You and worship at Your footstool; You are holy. I praise Your great and awesome name, for You are holy. There is no one holy like You; there is no one beside You. O Holy One, I will praise Your name, for Your name alone is exalted; Your splendor is above the earth and the heavens. (Ps. 11:4a; 113:5-6; 99:5, 3; 1 Sam. 2:2a; Ps. 148:13 paraphrased)

Prayers, Praises, and Personal Notes

_____

_____

_____

_____

_____

WEEK TWO

Receive God's Grace

"For it is by grace you have been saved,
through faith—and this not from yourselves,
it is the gift of God—not by works,
so that no one can boast."

EPHESIANS 2:8-9

*T*he flooded Amagu River was deeper, stronger, and more treacherous than Bob Conrad had anticipated. A missionary in Papua New Guinea, he had just completed a twelve-village visit in the East Sepik Province. Now he waited to cross the river, hoping the water would go down so he could return home.

After waiting more than an hour, he drove his motorbike to a place where he'd crossed the river many times before. He rode down the bank into the water, but the engine sputtered and died. Suddenly the swift current swept Bob downstream.

Still on his bike, he desperately tried to reach shore. Then he fell, and the bike pinned him underwater. He fought to reach the surface for air; but the raging river and the weight of his bike, backpack, helmet, and a heavily loaded string bag kept pulling him under.

Quickly losing strength, he prayed, "Lord, help me!"

A young man passing by saw Bob's plight and rushed down the riverbank. Benny Gabriel tried to pull the struggling man out of the water, but he couldn't do it alone. Then a surge of water from upstream swelled the tumultuous river, making it even more dangerous.

Three of Benny's friends arrived at the scene just then and rushed to help him. The men formed a human chain, linked hands, and pulled Bob ashore. Later the local people told Bob that it was the first time anyone had been caught in the floodwaters of the Amagu River and survived.[1]

Sanctifying Grace

Through this story we see a picture of Jesus' grace. Without Christ, we are caught in the world's floodwaters and dragged under by the heavy backpack of sin. Though we may struggle to reach safety by ourselves, the weight of sin will continue to pull us under. We do not have the strength to save ourselves.

When we cry out to the Lord to rescue us, He reaches down for us and carries us safely to shore. "Everyone who calls on the name of the Lord will be saved" (Rom. 10:13). But the Lord not only saves us, He also *sanctifies* us. Sanctification is a term much easier to define than to translate into our lives. For example, how would the word *computer* be translated into the native language of a people who have never seen a computer and have no electrical equipment? A picture of a computer would be meaningless to them.

Leading a holy life is similar to the difficulty of translating a word from one language into another. Holiness is a heavenly word that is difficult to comprehend. How do we translate it so it makes sense in our worldly language? How can we understand holiness in the context of our computerized, scientific, television age? How does being holy fit into our culture, lifestyles, and traditions? It doesn't fit at all. It never has.

The only way we'll begin to understand how to become holy is to realize that we do not belong to this world (John 15:19). We're aliens and strangers whose language, culture, and lifestyle should be different from those of the people who *do* belong. We're God's people and citizens of heaven (1 Peter 2:10-11; Phil. 3:20).

Christians are like immigrants who have left their homeland to reside in a foreign country. Many immigrants who come to America speak their native languages and carry on their own traditions. But if they desire to become citizens of this country, they must learn English, study United States government and history, and adapt to this country's culture and way of living.

As Christians, we are citizens of heaven, but our native country is this world. Often it seems easier to follow the world's ways than to learn the new language of holiness, to adopt godly ways, and to adapt to a whole new life in Christ.

How often do we follow God's holy ways one moment, but in the next moment our actions or thoughts may be horrifyingly sinful? How many of us confess a sin and vow we'll never do it again and then immediately commit that same sin? Our failure and sin rate may be so high that we doubt if we'll ever become the godly persons God desires us to be. Leading a holy life may seem so difficult that we give up trying.

But before giving up, consider a few saints. Moses murdered an Egyptian, fled to the desert, and spent forty years in exile herding sheep. Moses was so afraid when God appeared to him that he asked God to choose someone else to lead the Israelites.

David committed adultery with Bathsheba and devised a plan to have her husband murdered. Seventy thousand men of Israel died in a plague, because David conducted an unauthorized census of his troops.

The woman at the well was a prostitute who had five husbands, and she was not married to the man she was living with. Three times Peter betrayed Jesus by denying that he knew Him.

Saul of Tarsus persecuted Christians and consented to the stoning of Stephen. Paul confessed, "For I am the least of the apostles and do not even deserve to be called an apostle, because I persecuted the church of God. But by the grace of God I am what I am, and his grace to me was not without effect. No, I worked harder than all of them—yet not I, but the grace of God that was with me" (1 Cor. 15:9-10).

"By realizing that he did not deserve and could never earn the privileges given him, Paul was freed to be exactly who he was and do precisely what he was called to do. Grace became his silent partner, his constant traveling companion, his invisible security, since he (in himself) was in no way deserving of the part he played in God's unfolding drama."[2]

We are equally undeserving. Though we may keep falling, holiness calls us to repeated confession and repentance. Let us not be defeated by our guilt; instead, may it drive us to reconcile ourselves to Christ so we may be free to live by His grace.

Our hope is in this promise: "Where sin increased, grace increased all the more, so that, just as sin reigned in death, so also grace might reign through righteousness to bring eternal life through Jesus Christ our Lord" (Rom. 5:20b-21).

That does not mean we minimize sin in our lives. "What shall we say, then? Shall we go on sinning so that grace may increase? By no means!" (Rom. 6:1-2a). The Holy Spirit will strengthen us by the transforming power of God's amazing grace to overcome our darkest sins.

By divine grace we'll grow into godly persons. As we submit ourselves to God and yield our will to His, the holiness He desires of us will gradually come. We are responsible to live holy sanctified lives—continually dying to our sins, rising to newness of life, and being changed into God's image—yet we cannot do it without the grace of God working in us.

Cheap Grace Versus Costly Grace

Though we are responsible to lead godly separated lives, we are saved by grace not by works (Eph. 2:8). That truth is foundational to our Christian faith. We may feel driven to work hard for God and do everything and more in a church or ministry. Or we may think that since we are not saved by works, we're safe to do as we please because we'll get to heaven anyway. We may not openly admit that view, but we may demonstrate it by the way we live.

Here we confront the stark differences between "cheap grace" and "costly grace." "Cheap grace is the grace we bestow on ourselves. . . . Cheap grace is grace without discipleship, grace without the cross, grace without Jesus Christ, living and incarnate."[3]

We're living by cheap grace if we do whatever we please without any sense of responsibility to the Lord. If we remain in an apathetic spiritual condition and refuse to deal with our sins, we'll become hardened and insensitive to our need for constant spiritual renewal. If we keep resisting the Holy Spirit's conviction to change, we won't submit ourselves to the lifelong process of transformation. We won't be committed to a disciplined spiritual life, personal discipleship, and service. Christ may be our Savior, but He is not our Lord and Master. That's cheap grace!

"Costly grace is the gospel which must be *sought* again and again, the gift which must be *asked* for, the door at which a man must *knock*. Such grace is *costly* because it calls us to follow *Jesus Christ*. It is costly because it costs a man his life, and it is grace because it gives a man the only true life. It is costly because it condemns sin, and grace because it justifies the sinner. . . . Costly grace confronts us as a gracious call to follow Jesus; it comes as a word of forgiveness to the broken spirit and the contrite heart."[4]

Costly grace calls us to be transformed by the Holy Spirit's power and the Word of God throughout our entire lifetime. Costly grace holds us accountable to repent and change, to be more Christlike, more faithful and fruitful. Costly graces pushes us out of our comfortable places and challenges us to be daily open to opportunities to minister to others. Costly grace is sacrificial giving and living.

Grace for Weakness

Costly grace also means that God's strength is demonstrated and perfected in our weakness. "My grace is sufficient for you, for my power is made perfect in weakness" (2 Cor. 12:9a). I struggle with my own frailties and failures. Weaknesses and sins of all kinds plague me. I continually battle to overcome depression, worry, overeating, and overworking.

An extremely painful physical condition has flared up again, one that has plagued me off and on for thirty-nine years. The doctor said, "It's treatable but not curable." Despite constant medical treatments and my following a highly restricted regime, the pain persists. It's barely manageable, exhausts me, and limits my activities.

In a similar way, spiritual weaknesses and frailties may be treatable but not curable while we're here on earth. The pain caused by the consequences of having a fallen fleshly nature is excruciating and exhausting. The hurt may seem unmanageable and our effectiveness for God limited. Faithful obedience and submission to God is the only sure treatment that works, and it has to be administered time and again.

Few of us completely and diligently follow God's prescription for holiness. It's a daily battle for holiness against sin, sickness, and self. When we receive God's grace, we trust that He is sufficient even when we are deficient.

I appreciate Charles Swindoll's candid remarks on this subject, "Another undeniable struggle all of us live with is our own human weaknesses, which crop up any number of ways again and again. We suffer. We hurt. We fail. We blow it. We feel bad. Medication won't relieve it. Prayer doesn't remove it. Complaining doesn't help it. Our problem? We are just human! Imperfection dogs our steps."[5]

Heavenly Grace

Though we may suffer from imperfections, failure, and weakness, we may by God's grace look forward to a whole new life. "Our citizenship is in heaven. And we eagerly await a Savior from there, the Lord Jesus Christ, who, by the power that enables him to bring everything under his control, will transform our lowly bodies so that they will be like his glorious body" (Phil. 3:20-21). We will no longer be plagued by the addictions, ailments, sins, and weaknesses that weigh us down. What grace!

Here's a great promise to hold onto while we await that day. "'Behold, I will create new heavens and a new earth. The former things will not be remembered, nor will they come to mind'" (Isa. 65:17). When we reach heaven, we'll celebrate the pleasures of eternity without even the memory of our former earthly condition. We'll experience the joyous freedom of being holy forevermore. We'll live with our glorious Savior in a heavenly universe so vast and unknown to us we cannot begin to imagine the wonders awaiting us. That's grace!

Scripture Reading: Ephesians 2:1-7

Practicing the Spiritual Life

What condition are we in without Christ Jesus as our Savior? According to verses 4-7, what has God done for us?

_____

_____

_____

Make a commitment to stop gratifying a specific craving that is controlling your life. Then write a personal psalm affirming that you are alive in Christ because of God's great love, grace, and mercy for you.

_____

_____

_____

Prayer

O Holy God, deliver me all day and all night long from greedy coveting. Free me from having the soul and life of the wicked who craves and seeks evil, and who gives no favor or mercy to others. May I never boast of the cravings of my heart or bless the greedy, for in doing so I revile You, Lord. May I never boast except in Your cross, Lord Jesus Christ, through which the world has been crucified to me, and I to the world. (Prov. 21:26a KJV; Prov. 21:10 AMP; Ps. 10:3; Gal. 6:14 paraphrased)

Prayers, Praises, and Personal Notes

_____

_____

_____

_____

_____

Scripture Reading: Ephesians 2:8-10

Practicing the Spiritual Life

How are we saved?

_____

_____

_____

Though we are not saved by our works, costly grace calls us to do the work of God. Ask the Lord to show you a godly deed that you may do today.

_____

_____

_____

Prayer

I confess with my mouth, "Jesus, You are Lord," and I believe in my heart that God raised You from the dead, and I will be saved. For Your grace that brings salvation has appeared to me. Now I pray that I may live a life worthy of You, Lord, and may please You in every way—bearing fruit in every good work, growing in my knowledge of You. As You have commanded, I will do good, be rich in good deeds, and be generous and willing to share. In the same way, I will let my light shine before others, that they may see my good deeds and praise You, Father in heaven. (Rom. 10:9; Titus 2:11; Col. 1:10; 1 Tim. 6:18; Matt. 5:16 paraphrased)

Prayers, Praises, and Personal Notes

_____

_____

_____

_____

_____

Scripture Reading: Romans 5:12-19

Practicing the Spiritual Life

What do we receive by grace through Christ—in contrast to sin and death through Adam?

_____

_____

_____

What do you most appreciate about the costly gift of grace?

_____

_____

_____

Prayer

As in Adam I will die, even so in You, Jesus, I shall be made alive. You were handed over to die because of my sins, and You were raised from the dead to make me right with God. Therefore, since I have been made right in Your sight, O God, I have peace with You because of what You have done for me. Because of my faith, Jesus, You have brought me into this place of highest privilege where I now stand, and I confidently and joyfully look forward to sharing in Your glory. Until that day, may Your grace be poured out on me abundantly, along with faith and love for You, Christ Jesus. (1 Cor. 15:22 KJV; Rom. 4:25 NLT; 5:1-2 NLT; 1 Tim. 1:14 paraphrased)

Prayers, Praises, and Personal Notes

_____

_____

_____

_____

_____

Scripture Reading: Romans 5:20–6:2

Practicing the Spiritual Life

What is stronger than sin? What is our relationship with sin?

_____

_____

_____

What sins do you need to die to so that grace may rule your life?

_____

_____

_____

Prayer

Jesus, because I believe in You, I am freed from all guilt and declared right with God—something the Jewish law could not do. Therefore, sin shall not be my master, because I am not under law, but under grace. What then? Shall I sin because I am not under law but under grace? By no means! I will not set aside Your grace, for if righteousness could be gained through the law, Jesus, You died for nothing! (Acts 13:39 NLT; Rom. 6:14-15; Gal. 2:21 paraphrased)

Prayers, Praises, and Personal Notes

_____

_____

_____

_____

_____

_____

Scripture Reading: 1 Peter 5:5-11

Practicing the Spiritual Life

To whom does God give grace, and how do we demonstrate His grace? What are the ways we're to stand firm in our faith?

_____

_____

_____

Do you need to change any attitudes so that you may become a humble person of grace?

_____

_____

_____

Prayer

O my Servant Savior, by Your grace, by Your unmerited favor given to me, I will not esteem or think of myself more highly than I ought. I will not have an exaggerated opinion of my own importance, but will rate my ability with sober judgment, according to the degree of faith You apportioned to me. For You have shown me what is good and what You require of me—to act justly and to love mercy and to walk humbly with You, Lord. (Rom. 12:3 AMP; Micah 6:8 paraphrased)

Prayers, Praises, and Personal Notes

_____

_____

_____

_____

_____

Scripture Reading: John 17:15-21

Practicing the Spiritual Life

What did Jesus pray for His disciples and for all believers? How are we sanctified?

_____

_____

_____

In what ways do you need to live by the truth in order to lead a sanctified life?

_____

_____

_____

Prayer

From the beginning, O God, You chose me to be saved through the sanctifying work of Your Spirit and through belief in the truth. You called me to this through the Gospel that I might share in Your glory, Jesus. So then I will stand firm and hold to the teachings that were passed on to me. Lord Jesus Christ, may You and God my Father, who loves me and by Your grace gives me eternal encouragement and good hope, encourage my heart and strengthen me in every good deed and word. (2 Thess. 2:13b-17 paraphrased)

Prayers, Praises, and Personal Notes

_____

_____

_____

_____

_____

Scripture Reading: 2 Corinthians 12:7-10

Practicing the Spiritual Life

For what was God's grace sufficient in Paul's life? What did he boast about and delight in?

_____

_____

_____

For what weaknesses do you need Christ's powerful grace?

_____

_____

_____

Prayer

O God, Your foolishness is wiser than my wisdom, and Your weakness is stronger than my strength. I will remember what I was when I was called. I was not wise by human standards nor influential and powerful, nor of high and noble birth. For You chose the foolish things of the world to shame the wise; You chose the weak things of the world to shame the strong. You chose the lowly things of this world and the despised things—and the things that are not—to nullify the things that are, so that I may not boast before You. It is because of You that I am in Christ, who has become for me wisdom from You, O God—that is, my righteousness, holiness, and redemption. (1 Cor. 1:25-30 paraphrased)

Prayers, Praises, and Personal Notes

_____

_____

_____

_____

_____

_____

_____

_____

_____

_____

_____

_____

_____

_____

_____

_____

_____

_____

_____

_____

_____

_____

_____

_____

_____

_____

_____

WEEK THREE

Resolve to Win the War for Holiness

*"Fight the good fight of the faith.
Take hold of the eternal life
to which you were called
when you made your good confession
in the presence of many witnesses."*

1 TIMOTHY 6:12

When international armed forces were on a peacekeeping mission in Bosnia, they oversaw the peace accords between warring factions. One of the military peacekeepers' major tasks was mapping the more than 4,000 "belts" of minefields containing an estimated 1.5 to 4 million mines.

It was impossible to pinpoint all the minefields along enemy borders. Both sides had made crude maps that were difficult to decipher, and many of the maps had been thrown away. Soldiers from the warring countries had laid out land mines randomly instead of using the patterns they had learned in military training. Their strategy was to confuse and ultimately destroy their enemies.

In the vicinity of these minefields, soldiers and villagers dared not wander across the country or stray onto unknown roads; they had to stay on paved roads or areas that were marked safe. But even those areas were not really safe, since many mines had not been discovered.[1]

Warring armies were ordered to clear certain minefields in their own territories, but land mines were difficult to detect and dangerous to dismantle. Camouflaged mines were mounted above or laid on the ground; other mines were buried just beneath the surface of the earth. Mines were easily detonated when a person, animal, or vehicle brushed against a trip wire; or they were set off by the pressure of a footstep.[2] While trying to dismantle the explosives, many soldiers were killed when they accidentally detonated their own mines.[3]

This Bosnian war story and our own spiritual conflicts have many parallels. We experience random and senseless attacks from the Enemy that embroil us in warfare within and without. We are not alone in our ongoing spiritual battle. All persons since Adam and Eve have suffered combat casualties from their own sins and/or from the sins of others. But though we may lose skirmishes with sin, God has won the war.

Jesus took our place in the battle and in our stead devastated our archenemy sin at the cross, breaking its hold on us. We are actually *dead* to sin (Rom. 6:10-11).

Christ made it possible for us to lead a holy life, but it's our responsibility to resist sin.[4] He has commissioned us to serve as a member of a peace-keeping mission. We have been assigned the lifelong duty of overseeing peace accords between two warring factions, our old nature and the new. "You were taught, with regard to your former way of life, to put off your old self, which is being corrupted by its deceitful desires; to be made new in the attitude of your minds; and to put on the new self, created to be like God in true righteousness and holiness" (Eph. 4:22-24).

We must daily resolve to win the war for holiness. But how do we fight the battle?

Fallen and Wounded

Holiness requires us to recognize our condition as fallen, wounded people. The hard truth is that self-inflicted casualties among Christians are common. We may commit sins that have resulted in a serious financial, personal, or relational loss. We may have secret sins that we think we're hiding, or we may deceive ourselves about the seriousness of our wrongdoing.

We may be in denial about our spiritual condition and fortify ourselves against realistically facing our sins. We act as if we're leading a godly life even though we may be deep in sin and harming others at the same time. "If we say we have no sin, we are only fooling ourselves and refusing to accept the truth" (1 John 1:8 NLT).

We do not see ourselves and our sins as God and others see them. We do not know our own hearts or our potential for sin. "The heart is deceitful above all things and beyond cure. Who can understand it?" (Jer. 17:9). "Furthermore, we must never consider that our fight against sin is at an end. The heart is unsearchable, our evil desires are insatiable, and our reason is constantly in danger of being deceived."[5]

Since we do not truly know ourselves and are so easily deceived, let us ask the Spirit of God—who knows our hearts, motives, and secret intentions—to search and test them, to show us any self-deception and ungodly behaviors that we need to be delivered from. Let us daily ask Him to help us have pure thoughts, pure motives, and pure actions (Ps. 139:23-24).

Consequences

Holiness requires that we realistically understand the consequences of our wrong choices and our responsibility to God and others. We may think that if we fall in some major way, we can handle the disastrous outcome. If we do fall, we may minimize the amount of damage, rationalize the rightness of our destructive choices, and fortify ourselves against the heart-wrenching pain of those affected by our fall. We may also blame them for our own wrongdoing.

On the other hand, we may realize that we're in sin but feel as if we're weak, easily defeated, and don't have the strength to change. We may even feel that God has failed to help us and question why He doesn't give us the power we need to overcome habitual sins.

Yet Scripture clearly states: "There hath no temptation taken you but such as is common to man: but God is faithful, who will not suffer you to be tempted above that ye are able; but will with the temptation also make a way to escape, that ye may be able to bear it" (1 Cor. 10:13 KJV).

"The Christian should never complain of want of ability and power. If we sin, it is because we chose to sin, not because we lack the ability to say no to temptation. It is time for us Christians to face up to our responsibility for holiness. Too often we say we are 'defeated' by this or that sin. No, we are not defeated; we are simply disobedient!"[6]

Moreover, we may get away with our sins and go many years without serious repercussions. We delude ourselves into believing that God won't call us to account. We think He has forgotten and does not see us because we have not experienced the consequences (Ps. 10:11, 13). The Lord, however, sees everything we do. He is observing our lives and examining our ways (Ps. 11:4b).

When we finally bear the consequences, they're often far more painful than we ever imagined. The wounds may be so deep that we or those who were injured may never be the same again. We may have to live with the devastating outcome our entire lives.

Ultimately, the Lord will hold us accountable and responsible for our wrongdoing. How much wiser to realistically confront our sins, repent of them, and clear those explosive mines from our lives by the powerful grace of our forgiving Savior. This is our greatest hope. The Lord is kind, merciful, and loving; He will restore us and redeem our broken lives. Even when we have nothing left but ashes and have to rebuild in a different place, we can start over again with a whole new life in Christ.

Victory Versus Obedience

Holiness requires us to appropriate God's attitude toward our sins. "Our first problem is that our attitude toward sin is more self-centered than God-centered. We are more concerned about our own 'victory' over sin than we are about the fact that our sins grieve the heart of God. We cannot tolerate failure in our struggle with sin chiefly because we are success-oriented, not because we know it is offensive to God. . . . God wants us to walk in *obedience*—not victory. Obedience is oriented toward God; victory is oriented toward self."[7]

We may also desire victory because we don't want to be caught or embarrassed. Our motive may be to preserve our reputation more than God's.

Above all, we need to grasp the reality that our sins offend the Lord. Gordon MacDonald said this about his own adulterous experience: "I've come to a high point of sensitivity about broken-world people, for I am a part of those who look back into their personal history and recall with strong regret an act or a series of acts that have resulted in great distress for themselves and many others. And what is worse is the fact that such performances are a terrible offense to God."[8]

We need to be more concerned about how we honor and glorify the Lord before others. How many people have been turned off to the truth of the gospel message because of the ungodly behavior of Christians?

The Lord's will is that we gain victory over our sins by His enabling power and our humble cooperation and obedience. "As we concentrate on living an obedient, holy life, we will certainly experience the joy of victory over sin."[9]

The Inward Battle

Holiness requires us to fight an inward battle to overcome our sins. Land mines beneath the surface or buried deep inside us have the potential of exploding and crippling ourselves and others. To maintain moral and spiritual integrity, we need to continually deal with these tendencies. We need to take God's help to conquer the darker forces that entice us to self-destruct.

"Not many people like to talk about this dimension of our inner selves, and our very ignorance or neglect of it may portend our vulnerability to brokenness. If God whispers, evil often shouts, and personal worlds break when that shouting gets our attention."[10]

Our inmost self—our appetites, cravings, and strong will—shouts for our attention and wars against sound, godly reasoning. When we give into those cravings and lusts, we lose the battle and feel defeated.

By our disobedience, we become a prisoner of our addictions and our thirst to have more and more. These don't come from God but from the world: the lust of the flesh, the insatiable craving for alcohol, drugs, food, and sensual gratification; the lust of the eyes, greedy desires for material goods and luxuries; the pride of life, being obsessed about having an attractive image and bodily appearance, attaining a certain status, and relying on our own abilities, reputation, and resources instead of God's (1 John 2:16).

"The crucial question then is, 'How do we destroy the strength and vitality of sin?' If we are to work at this difficult task, we must first have *conviction*. We must be persuaded that a holy life of God's will for every Christian is important. We must believe that the pursuit of holiness is worth the effort and pain required to mortify the misdeeds of the body."[11]

We need to open our hearts to the convicting power of the Holy Spirit if we're going to overcome sin. The Spirit is speaking to us about specific areas of sin in our lives; the problem is, we often dismiss His convicting voice and do as we please. We know exactly what the Lord has warned us to stop doing or what He desires us to do in the way of serving Him. Conviction is not always about sin; it may be about how we're to serve Him. If we have deluded ourselves, hardened our hearts, or are in denial, the Spirit won't be able to convict us at all.

The Outward Battle

Holiness requires us to fight an outward battle with sin. "We may think we merely respond to outward temptations that are presented to us. But the truth is, our evil desires are constantly searching out temptations to satisfy their insatiable lusts. Consider the particular temptations to which you are especially vulnerable, and note how often you find yourself searching out occasions to satisfy those evil desires."[12]

We may not think of our desires as evil; they are just simply things we enjoy. But are they? Can we live without them, or are we so addicted to our pleasures that we go through withdrawal when we try to go without them?

One afternoon, I was in a computer superstore that reminded me of a frenzied stock market exchange. I watched customers frantically perusing the newest equipment and programs or waiting in long lines for one of the twenty or more checkers to raise their numbered sign so buyers could purchase their cartloads of computer goods.

I was quickly caught up by the buying frenzy as I checked out color printers and multifunction fax machines. Though shoppers may have been buying what they needed and could afford, I felt strongly enticed to buy equipment I could not afford. Though I only bought the items on my list, I struggled with my own temptation.

How often do we give in to our compulsions and buy things we don't need, rarely use, and that deepen our debt level? How often do we win or lose our battle with seemingly good but wrong desires?

We must guard against carelessly wandering through enemy territory, because we're in danger of setting off explosive mines. Those land mines are camouflaged, and unless we're watchful, we won't see them. If we trigger a mine and it blows up, the damage will be extensive and visible.

The way to win the inward and outward battle is to be self-controlled, alert, and aware at all times of the Enemy's strategies. He's constantly patrolling our lives to find a break in our spiritual defenses so that he may seize us and make us captive to sin.

During our daily journeys, we must watch for danger zones. We must wear our spiritual armor and guard our actions and behavior. We must run swiftly from temptation, be alert to our own enticing desires that lead us onto the wide road of sin, stay on the narrow road, the one that has been marked safe and leads to life (Matt. 7:13-14). That road is Christ Himself.

God's Provisions

Holiness calls us to rely on God's provisions for leading a godly life. "He makes provision for our holiness, but He gives us the responsibility to use those provisions."[13]

We have the full armor of God to win our battles against sin and the devil's schemes. Stand firm with the belt of truth, breastplate of righteousness, shield of faith, helmet of salvation, and sword of the Spirit, which is God's mighty Word (Eph. 6:11, 14-17). Overcome sin through fasting, prayer, the empowering work of God's indwelling Spirit, and accountability to other Christians.

God's provisions through Christ Jesus are abundant. Because Jesus took our place on the cross, we possess a new identity as forgiven, cleansed people. "In him we have redemption through his blood, the forgiveness of sins, in accordance with the riches of God's grace" (Eph. 1:7).

Through faith in Christ, we're new, righteous people. "God made him who had no sin to be sin for us, so that in him we might become the righteousness of God" (2 Cor. 5:21).

God's provision of righteousness means we no longer have to be slaves to sin. Paul wrote to the Christians in Rome, "Thank God! Once you were slaves of sin, but now you have obeyed with all your heart the new teaching God has given you. Now you are free from sin, your old master, and you have become slaves to your new master, righteousness. . . . Now you must choose to be slaves of righteousness so that you will become holy" (Rom. 6:17-18, 19b NLT).

When we choose to be a slave of righteousness, we're freed to experience the depths of God's love, the peace of His abiding presence, and the joy of His transforming power in our lives. We are filled with the fruit of righteousness that comes through Christ and brings God glory and praise (Phil. 1:11).

As we see ourselves as new people in Christ, we can believe that we are truly dead to sin and alive to God. "What is the significance of being alive unto God? How does it help us in our pursuit of holiness? For one thing, it means we are united with Christ in all His power."[14]

We have inherited God's incomparably great power in Christ. That power is like the work of God's mighty strength when He raised Jesus from the dead and appointed Him to be the head over everything (Eph. 1:18-22). Imagine how God could demonstrate His power through us if we totally surrendered ourselves to Him.

Scripture Reading: Ephesians 4:22-32

Practicing the Spiritual Life
What attitudes and actions of the old self are we to put off?

_____

_____

_____

From this passage do you find any old ways of acting or thinking that you need to take off and get rid of?

_____

_____

_____

Prayer
Spirit of holiness, strengthen me to kill, deaden, and deprive the power of evil desires lurking in my members, those animal impulses and all that is earthly in me that is sin: sexual vice, impurity, sensual appetites, unholy desires, and all greed and covetousness, for that is idolatry and the lifting up of self and other created things instead of You, God. I will now rid myself of all these things: anger, rage, malice, slander, and filthy language. I will not lie to others, since I have taken off my old self with its practices and have put on my new self, which is being renewed in knowledge in Your image, O my Creator. (Col. 3:5 AMP; Col. 3:8-10 paraphrased)

Prayers, Praises, and Personal Notes

_____

_____

_____

_____

Scripture Reading: Ephesians 4:22-32

Practicing the Spiritual Life

As you read yesterday's passage again, note the ways we are to put on the new self and become holy.

_____

_____

_____

What new attitudes and actions do you need to put on?

_____

_____

_____

Prayer

Merciful and loving Lord, I will clothe myself, as Your chosen one, who is purified and holy and well beloved by You. I'll put on behavior marked by tenderhearted compassion and mercy, kind feelings, a lowly opinion of myself, gentle ways, and patience, which is tireless, long-suffering, and has the power to endure whatever comes, with good temper. I will be gentle and forbearing with others, and if I have a complaint, difference, or grievance against someone, I will readily pardon that person; even as You, Lord, freely forgave me, so I must also forgive. And the most important piece of clothing I must wear is love. Love is what binds me with others in perfect harmony. (Col. 3:12-13 AMP; Col. 3:14 NLT paraphrased)

Prayers, Praises, and Personal Notes

_____

_____

_____

_____

Scripture Reading: 1 John 1:5–2:6

Practicing the Spiritual Life

In what ways do we deceive ourselves about our sin? How are we to live and walk as Christians?

_____

_____

_____

Ask the Lord to reveal your true spiritual condition. What steps will you take to start walking in the light and in truth?

_____

_____

_____

Prayer

Light of the world, I will put aside the deeds of darkness and put on the armor of light. For though my heart was once full of darkness, now I am full of light from You, Lord, and my behavior should show it. For this light within me produces only what is good and right and true. I will try to find out what is pleasing to You. I will take no part in the worthless deeds of evil and darkness; instead, I'll rebuke and expose them. True instruction will be in my mouth, and nothing false will be found on my lips. I will walk with You in peace and uprightness and turn many from sin. (Rom. 13:12b; Eph. 5:8-11 NLT; Mal. 2:6 paraphrased)

Prayers, Praises, and Personal Notes

_____

_____

_____

_____

Scripture Reading: Romans 7:14–8:4

Practicing the Spiritual Life

What did Paul say about his failure to do good and to win the inward and outward battle with evil? How are we set free from sin?

_____

_____

_____

Are you ever discouraged by failure to win the battle against sin?

_____

_____

_____

Prayer

O Holy God, though I was indeed called to freedom, I will not let my freedom be an incentive to my flesh as an excuse for selfishness. I will walk and live habitually in Your Spirit, responsive to and guided by Your Spirit; then I will certainly not gratify the cravings and desires of my flesh. For my sinful nature desires what is contrary to Your Spirit, and Your Spirit what is contrary to my sinful nature. They are in conflict with each other, so that I do not do what I want. Rather, I will clothe myself with You, Lord Jesus; I will not think about how to gratify the desires of my sinful nature. (Gal. 5:13a, 16 AMP; Gal. 5:17; Rom. 13:14 paraphrased)

Prayers, Praises, and Personal Notes

_____

_____

_____

_____

_____

Scripture Reading: James 4:1-10

Practicing the Spiritual Life

What are some of the causes of our inward and outward battle with sin?

_____

_____

_____

How did this passage speak to you about your own spiritual battle?

_____

_____

_____

Prayer

Loving Lord, as Your servant, I will not quarrel; instead, I will be kind to everyone. I will think of ways to encourage others to outbursts of love and good deeds. Now I submit myself to You and will be at peace with You. I draw near to You with a sincere heart in full assurance of faith, having my heart sprinkled to cleanse myself from a guilty conscience and having my body washed with pure water. I will purify myself from everything that contaminates body and spirit, perfecting holiness out of reverence for You, O God. (2 Tim. 2:24a; Heb. 10:24 NLT; Job 22:21a; Heb. 10:22; 2 Cor. 7:1b paraphrased)

Prayers, Praises, and Personal Notes

_____

_____

_____

_____

_____

Scripture Reading: Numbers 12

Practicing the Spiritual Life
What did Aaron and Miriam do against their brother Moses, and what were the consequences?

_____

_____

_____

Are you experiencing the consequences of your sin or someone else's sin? If so, what do you believe the Lord would have you do?

_____

_____

_____

Prayer
God of all wisdom, may I not bring woe onto myself by thinking I am wise in my own eyes and clever in my own sight. For if I think I am something when I am nothing, I deceive myself. I will test my own actions. Then I can take pride in myself without comparing myself to someone else. I won't be impressed with my own wisdom. Instead, I'll fear You, Lord, and turn my back on evil. For the greatest among others is Your servant, Lord. (Isa. 5:21; Gal. 6:3-4; Prov. 3:7 NLT; Matt. 23:11 paraphrased)

Prayers, Praises, and Personal Notes

_____

_____

_____

_____

_____

Scripture Reading: 1 Samuel 15:10-31

Practicing the Spiritual Life

How did Saul rationalize his disobedience? Though Saul seemed sorry about his sin, what was he more concerned about? (v. 30)

Is there any area of your life where you are more concerned about appearances than obedience? If so, what will you change?

Prayer

Lord of Righteousness, I pray that I may have a pure heart, for to the pure, all things are pure, but if I am corrupted and do not believe, nothing is pure. In fact, both my mind and my conscience would be corrupted. I will not claim to know You, God, if my actions deny that I know You. For then I would be disobedient and unfit for doing anything good. I will not flatter You with my mouth or lie to You with my tongue; for if I did, my heart would not be loyal to You, nor would I be faithful to Your covenant. I will not swear falsely by Your name and so profane Your name, O God. You are the Lord! (Titus 1:15-16; Ps. 78:36-37; Lev. 19:12 paraphrased)

Prayers, Praises, and Personal Notes

WEEK FOUR

Revere God's Holy Attributes

"It is the Lord your God you must follow,
and him you must revere.
Keep his commands and obey him;
serve him and hold fast to him."

DEUTERONOMY 13:4

*M*y homesickness surprised me. We had anticipated moving to Santa Maria for such a long time, and now we were living close to our sons and their families. I loved my new home, but I felt a restless longing to return to Orange County where we had lived for most of our married life.

One weekend I went back for a visit. It eased my homesickness to drive through our neighborhood and see family, friends, and other familiar places. When I went to our old house to pick up mail, the Hispanic family living there warmly welcomed me and insisted on giving me a tour. It was the first house they had ever bought. The mother talked to me in Spanish as she took me through every room. Though I barely understood her, I saw how pleased she was to have her own home.

The father had been a migrant worker and was now a ranch foreman. As Andre, their grown son, showed me how his father had turned the yard into a fruit orchard and garden, he proudly named every tree and vegetable. I left with a bag of luscious tomatoes and a feeling of joy that this family was living in our old house.

Knowing God

God not only created us to be homesick for loved ones and home but for Himself and heaven. "You have made us for yourself, and our heart is restless until it rests in you."[1]

As we journey toward holiness, we come to realize our deep longing to know the Lord more personally. Who is this God who has pursued, wooed, and won us? This Lover of our Souls—what is He like?

"There is but one only living and true God, who is infinite in being and perfection, a most pure spirit . . . immutable, immense, eternal . . . almighty, most wise, most holy, most free, most absolute . . . most loving, gracious, merciful, long-suffering, abundant in goodness and truth, forgiving iniquity, transgression and sin; the rewarder of them that diligently seek him. . . . "[2]

God is eternal and self-existent; therefore, He is self-sufficient. He does not depend on anyone or anything, as we must do, to survive.

He is infinite in being, which means He has no beginning or ending. He does not age or grow more mature or wiser. God is eternal and immense; therefore, He must possess all knowledge, all power, and all wisdom; and all His attributes must essentially exist in their unlimited fullness.[3]

God is always the same. He can never be unfaithful or unloving because that would require Him to change. He is immutable, which means He is unchanging. He can never change for better or worse as we do. Any defect in the character of God would mean that He is imperfect, which He can never be. God is holy, infinite in perfection, and a most pure spirit.[4]

Since we humans constantly change and contradict ourselves, it is difficult for us to conceive of someone who doesn't. God is in complete harmony and agreement with Himself. His justice does not contradict His mercy; His judgment of the lost does not contradict His forgiveness and grace to the redeemed.[5]

The Lord our God is one God, but He relates to us in many different and distinct capacities. He is the Creator of the universe, our Father and Provider who meets all of our needs.

Jesus, our Savior, identified with us by coming to us in human flesh and demonstrating His healing compassion and love. He understands and cares about our earthly concerns, needs, and problems. He is our Redeemer, and through Him we have eternal life.

The Holy Spirit convicts and delivers us from sin. He indwells us, is ever-present, ever-caring, and meets our deepest heart cries, which no other human being can do for us. He is our Comforter and Counselor who guides us. The Holy Spirit empowers us to serve the Lord and enables us to use our spiritual gifts.

God Is Loving

Our greatest personal need is to know God's love. Our deepest spiritual need is to love the Lord with all our heart and all our soul and all our strength (Deut. 6:5). I have seen a glimpse of godly love in a few Christian couples who have been married for many years. They have a oneness and tender affection that is inspiring. Though they experienced numerous hardships, their commitment and devotion to the Lord and to each other has been strengthened by their adversities.

If we're going to remain faithful to the Lord, God's love must be more than a statement in our theology. It must be something we know in the depths of our heart. First, we may be assured that our Lord loves us as passionately as a groom loves his bride. Jesus unites with us spiritually in holy love. He is a faithful husband. We, too, must vow to join ourselves with our most Beloved, as a bride to her groom. As we remain faithful and our love for the Lord grows stronger over time, as we remain spiritually steadfast in adversity, we will develop a deep oneness with Him and a steadfast assurance of His love.

Second, "because God is self-sufficient, His love had no beginning; because He is eternal, His love can have no end; because He is infinite, it has no limit . . . because He is immense, His love is an incomprehensibly vast, bottomless, shoreless sea before which we kneel in joyful silence. . . . "[6]

Third, nothing or no one in heaven or on earth can separate us from the love of Christ. We may feel separated from Him and question His love when we experience heartaches and troubles. We may feel as if the measure of God's love is the abundance of blessings we receive and that terrible trials are His way of withholding love and punishing us for our sins. God *is love*; therefore, He cannot withhold His love.

"The Lord disciplines those he loves, and he punishes everyone he accepts as a son." "God disciplines us for our good, that we may share in his holiness" (Heb. 12:6, 10). As an example, Joseph was sold by his own brothers into slavery, falsely accused of a crime, and sent to prison, where he seemed to be forgotten. God allowed Joseph to be disciplined for a dual purpose, so he could become spiritually mature and trained for ministry. Joseph saved his own family, who were God's chosen people, and the Egyptians from starvation during a famine.[7]

No matter what hardships we experience, God loves us. He has not and will not forsake us. Danger, famine, hardship, persecution, trouble, loss of everything, and even the threat of death cannot separate us from Christ's love (Rom. 8:35). "I am convinced that neither death nor life, neither angels nor demons, neither the present nor the future, nor any powers, neither height nor depth, nor anything else in all creation, will be able to separate us from the love of God that is in Christ Jesus our Lord" (Rom. 8:38-39).

God Is Most Holy

We have a deep need to know that God is holy and untouched by sin. God's holiness provides us with absolute security and restrains Satan from utterly destroying us.

"Holy is the way God is. To be holy, He does not conform to a standard. He is that standard. He is absolutely holy with an infinite, incomprehensible fullness of purity that is incapable of being other than it is. Because He is holy, His attributes are holy. . . . "[8]

It was a holy God who sent His Son to sacrifice His life for us that we may partake of His holiness. "For God so loved the world, that he gave his only begotten Son, that whosoever believeth in him should not perish, but have everlasting life. For God sent not his Son into the world to condemn the world; but that the world through him might be saved" (John 3:16-17 KJV).

"Here God's holiness is seen in that He loves righteousness in the life of His children to such a degree that He gave His only begotten Son to secure it. The Cross shows how much God loves holiness. The Cross stands for God's holiness before even His love. For Christ died not merely for our sins, but in order that He might provide us with that righteousness of life which God loves."[9]

"Above all we must believe that God sees us perfect in His Son while He disciplines and chastens and purges us that we may be partakers of His holiness."[10] To be pure in heart, to lead a godly life, and to have spiritual power, we need to submit ourselves to God's discipline that we may know His holiness.[11]

God Is Always the Same

We have a deep need for the assurance that God does not change and is completely reliable. The owner of a large company that I once worked for did not trust his employees and was so changeable and inconsistent that we could not figure out what pleased him or provoked his displeasure. We felt insecure, and wasted a great deal of energy and productiveness trying to meet his unpredictable expectations.

On the other hand, I taught at a college where my supervisors were consistent and reliable and clearly communicated their expectations. They constantly expressed confidence and trust in their staff. We gladly worked overtime and were far more committed and productive because we felt appreciated and secure.

In the same way, we can totally rely on God to be consistent, reliable, and unchangeable. "Jesus Christ is the same yesterday and today and forever" (Heb. 13:8). God's nature is absolutely unchangeable. God is always the same. He does not grow or develop or vary from Himself in any way.[12] God is who He says He is. What He has promised He will perform. He keeps His word.

We are changeable people, however, because we possess the God-given power to think and act as we please. This freedom to change for good or bad may seem to be a curse, because the sins we humans commit result in so much suffering. But the freedom to change is in reality a blessing.

"In a fallen world such as this, the very ability to change is a golden treasure, a gift from God of such fabulous worth as to call for constant thanksgiving. For human beings the whole possibility of redemption lies in the ability to change. To move across from one sort of person to another is the essence of repentance: the liar becomes truthful, the thief honest, the lewd pure, the proud humble. The whole moral texture of the life is altered. The thoughts, the desires, the affections are transformed. . . . "[13]

God Is Merciful and Long-suffering

We have a deep need to know that God is merciful and long-suffering. "But when the kindness and love of God our Savior appeared, he saved us, not because of righteous things we had done, but because of his mercy" (Titus 3:4-5a).

God's mercy is infinite and inexhaustible; therefore, we need not fear that God will ever be unmerciful. Jesus Himself demonstrated the compassionate mercy of God in His ministry here on earth.

"God is merciful as well as just. He has always dealt in mercy with mankind and will always deal in justice when His mercy is despised. . . . We must believe that God's mercy is boundless, free, and, through Jesus Christ our Lord, available to us now in our present situation."[14]

God is also long-suffering; this means He is slow to anger and demonstrates patience and self-restraint in the face of provocation. "The Lord does not delay and be tardy or slow about what He promises, according to some people's conception of slowness, but He is long-suffering (extraordinarily patient) toward you, not desiring that any should perish, but that all should turn to repentance" (2 Peter 3:9 AMP).

Though we may fall often and wonder if we will overcome our habitual sins, God is long-suffering, abundantly merciful, and ready to forgive (Ps. 86:15). We are to pray boldly for God's forgiveness, mercy, and help for all our needs, sins, and weaknesses (Heb. 4:16). For He is surely willing to deliver us from sin and gives us the strength we need to repent and change.

God Is Ever Present

We have a deep need to experience the constant abiding presence of God. We desire closeness in human relationships, but no one can be with us at all times as God is.

He watches over us and is with us wherever we go. He sees everything we do and knows our every thought. He knows everything that happens to us, both good and evil. Surely, the Lord our Shepherd is guiding us through the darkest valleys, deepest rivers, and fiery trials. His thoughts of us are precious and so constant we cannot count them, for they number far more than all the grains of sand in the world (Ps. 139; Isa. 43:2).

What great comfort to know that God is constantly watching over us and listening to us. If we are Christians, His Spirit dwells within us. No one is as close to us as the Spirit of God or cares more about us. He is with us, within us, and will be with us always (Matt. 28:20).

God Is Faithful

We have a deep need to know the faithfulness of God. One of the deepest hurts we may experience is the wound of unfaithfulness. Once we have been betrayed, it is difficult to trust again; but we may rely on God's faithfulness even when others fail us.

"Know therefore that the Lord your God is God; he is the faithful God, keeping his covenant of love to a thousand generations of those who love him and keep his commands" (Deut. 7:9). God is always faithful, but He expects us to love and obey Him, and as we do, we may depend upon Him.

"Upon God's faithfulness rests our whole hope of future blessedness. Only as He is faithful will His covenants stand and His promises be honored. Only as we have complete assurance that He is faithful may we live in peace and look forward with assurance to the life to come."[15]

God Is Eternal

We have a deep need to live forever with God. Pyramids, monuments, and statues have been erected as eternal memorials to kings, queens, presidents, heroes, and heroines. Though the world tries to preserve their legacy, they will all be forgotten (Eccl. 1:11).

Rather than revering the memory of human heroes, let us exalt our eternal God. "Everything God does will endure forever; nothing can be added to it and nothing taken from it. God does it so that men will revere him" (Eccl. 3:14).

"Because God lives in an everlasting now, He has no past and no future. When time-words occur in the Scriptures, they refer to our time, not to His."[16] Though we are bound by time here on earth, we are actually living in eternity. Therefore, let us lift our eyes to the heavens and praise and worship our Lord God, who is from everlasting to everlasting.

God Is Our Rewarder

We have a deep need to know that God will reward us for remaining faithful to Him. "But without faith it is impossible to please him: for he that cometh to God must believe that he is, and that he is a rewarder of them that diligently seek him" (Heb. 11:6 KJV).

When we walk by faith and continually seek His guidance, no matter what difficulties we may experience, we have the confidence that He will reward us for trusting Him. We will be commended for our faith even if we do not see some of our most God-honoring requests answered.

For God has planned something far better for us than what this earth holds (Heb. 11:29-30). Jesus is preparing a place for us, an eternal home in heaven where we will enjoy the rewards of dwelling forever with Him (John 14:2-3).

Scripture Reading: 1 John 4:7-12

Practicing the Spiritual Life

How did God show His love for us?

_____

_____

_____

To whom can you show God's love in a special way today?

_____

_____

_____

Prayer

Heavenly Father, You demonstrated Your own love to me in this: While I was still a sinner, Christ died for me. For, God, You so greatly loved and dearly prized me that You gave up Your only begotten Son. I believe in, trust in, cling to, and rely on You, Jesus, so that I shall not perish and be lost, but have eternal life. For, God, You did not send Your Son in order to reject and condemn me, but that I might find salvation and be made safe through Jesus my Savior. This is how I know what love is: Jesus Christ, You laid down Your life for me. And I ought to lay down my life for others. I will love others as You have loved me. (Rom. 5:8; John 3:16-17 AMP; 1 John 3:16; John 15:12b paraphrased)

Prayers, Praises, and Personal Notes

_____

_____

_____

_____

_____

Scripture Reading: Isaiah 6:1-5; 57:15

Practicing the Spiritual Life

God is most holy. How did Isaiah respond when he saw the Lord God Almighty? Where and with whom does God live?

_____

_____

_____

How would you respond if you saw the Lord as Isaiah did?

_____

_____

_____

Prayer

"Who is like You, O Lord, glorious in holiness, awesome in splendor, doing wonders?" I exalt You, Lord God, and worship at Your holy place, for You are holy. I worship You in the splendor of Your holiness. Great and wonderful are Your deeds, Lord God Almighty! Just and true are Your ways, O King of the ages! Who shall not fear and glorify Your name? For You alone are holy. All nations shall come and worship You. Blessed be Your glorious name forever; may Your glory fill the whole earth! Amen and Amen! (Ex. 15:11b AMP not paraphrased; Ps. 99:9; 96:9a; Rev. 15:3b-4a; Ps. 72:19 RSV paraphrased)

Prayers, Praises, and Personal Notes

_____

_____

_____

_____

Scripture Reading: Deuteronomy 32:3-4; Hebrews 5:7-10; 2 Corinthians 13:11

Practicing the Spiritual Life

In what ways is God infinite in perfection? How was His Son made perfect?

_____

_____

_____

Perfection means completeness. Are there any areas of your spiritual life where you need to be more mature in Christ?

_____

_____

_____

Prayer

Author and Perfecter of my faith, Your way is perfect; Your Word is flawless. You are my shield, and I will take refuge in You. For who is God besides You, Lord? Who is the Rock except You? You arm me with strength and make my way perfect. Therefore, I am convinced that You who began a good work in me will continue developing that good work, perfecting and bringing it to full completion. And I pray, O God, that I may stand perfect and complete in all Your will. (2 Sam. 22:31-33; Phil. 1:6 AMP; Col. 4:12b KJV paraphrased)

Prayers, Praises, and Personal Notes

_____

_____

_____

_____

Scripture Reading: 1 Samuel 15:29; James 1:17

Practicing the Spiritual Life
What do these verses say about God's unchanging nature?

_____

_____

_____

In what areas of your life do you need the encouragement that God never changes?

_____

_____

_____

Prayer
Sovereign Lord, the One who never changes, Your plans stand firm forever, the purposes of Your heart through all generations. "In the beginning you laid the foundations of the earth, and the heavens are the work of your hands. They will perish, but you remain; they will all wear out like a garment. Like clothing you will change them and they will be discarded. But you remain the same, and your years will never end." (Ps. 33:22 paraphrased; Ps. 102:25-27 not paraphrased)

Prayers, Praises, and Personal Notes

_____

_____

_____

_____

_____

Scripture Reading: 1 Timothy 1:12-16

Practicing the Spiritual Life

God is merciful. What kind of man was Paul before he was saved? For what reason did God show Paul mercy?

_____

_____

_____

In what ways can you relate to Paul's condition before he believed in Christ? What does God's mercy mean to you?

_____

_____

_____

Prayer

O merciful Lord, remember Your tender mercies and Your lovingkindnesses; for they have been from everlasting. Remember not the sins of my youth nor my transgressions; according to Your mercy remember me for Your goodness' sake. For Your name's sake, O Lord, pardon mine iniquity and my guilt, for they are great. Rebuke me not in Your anger, nor chasten me in Your hot displeasure. Have mercy upon me, for I am weak and faint. My soul is also sorely troubled. Return, O Lord, deliver my soul; oh, save me for Your mercies' sake and Your steadfast love. (Ps. 25:6-7, 11 KJV, RSV; 6:1, 2a, 3a, 4 KJV and RSV paraphrased)

Prayers, Praises, and Personal Notes

_____

_____

_____

Scripture Reading: Deuteronomy 4:39; Hebrews 4:13

Practicing the Spiritual Life
God is ever present. What does He see and know about us?

_____

_____

_____

In what ways will you be more accountable to God, who sees everything we do?

_____

_____

_____

Prayer
Great are You, Lord, and of great power; Your understanding is inexhaustible and boundless. Your eyes are in every place, keeping watch upon the evil and the good. Your eyes are also on my ways; You see my every step. My ways are directly before Your eyes, and You—who would have me live soberly, chastely, and godly—carefully weigh all my goings. "Teach me to do Your will, for You are my God; let Your good Spirit lead me into a plain country and into the land of uprightness." (Ps. 147:5 AMP; Prov. 15:3 AMP; Job 34:21 AMP; Prov. 5:21 AMP paraphrased; Ps. 143:10 AMP not paraphrased)

Prayers, Praises, and Personal Notes

_____

_____

_____

_____

_____

Scripture Reading: 1 Corinthians 3:9-15; Revelation 22:12

Practicing the Spiritual Life

How do we build a solid foundation so that we may receive God's reward? For what will we be rewarded?

_____

_____

_____

What kind of spiritual foundation are you building?

_____

_____

_____

Prayer

Savior of the poor and needy, I will be careful not to do "acts of righteousness" before people, to be seen by them. If I do, I will have no reward from You, Father in heaven. So when I give to the needy, I will not announce it as the hypocrites do in the churches and on the streets, to be honored by people. The truth is, they have received their reward in full. But when I give to the needy, I will not let my left hand know what my right hand is doing, so that my giving may be in secret. Then, Father, You who see what is done in secret will reward me. For, Son of Man, You are going to come in Your Father's glory with Your angels, and then You will reward me according to what I have done. (Matt. 6:1-4; 16:27 paraphrased)

Prayers, Praises, and Personal Notes

_____

_____

_____

_____

WEEK FIVE

Recognize Life's Uncertainties

"'For I know the plans I have for you,' declares the Lord,
'plans to prosper you and not to harm you,
plans to give you hope and a future.
Then you will call upon me and come
and pray to me, and I will listen to you.
You will seek me and find me
when you seek me with all your heart.'"

JEREMIAH 29:11-13

*O*ne early June evening, blinding sunlight streamed into my car window. I felt tense as I tried to focus on the road and the mass of moving vehicles. I was traveling from Orange County to Santa Maria, more than a three-hour drive from southern to mid-state California.

It had been a two-day turnaround trip jammed with appointments and visits with family. I was tired and on the verge of an infection, though I didn't realize it at the time. All I could think about was getting home.

I decided to drive straight through without stopping. It was seven o'clock, and I figured the after-work traffic would quiet down from a roaring growl to a tame snarl. But when I reached Long Beach, traffic was deadlocked. I was going to be inching my way up the freeway if I didn't take a detour.

I was near a freeway that would take me into central Los Angeles and through the most dangerous part of that city, but traffic was moving. I prayed for safety and took the alternate route. I was greatly relieved when I passed out of the dangerous area and into more familiar territory.

Later, when I approached my usual turnoff where I take a fast food break and work out some of the road-wearying knots, I ignored the gentle nudging to stop. As I passed familiar rest areas, I kept ignoring the Holy Spirit's quiet prompting to take a break.

By the time I was about forty minutes from home, it was dark. I was super weary, dreaming of my own bed and a good night's rest. But when I came around the next bend, a bright red neon sign blinked at me: Detour! Detour! Detour!

Highway 101 was closed. I later learned that a large section of the road had slid into a sinkhole at a construction site. Within seconds, I found myself on the two-lane Highway One—winding, treacherous, and totally unfamiliar.

I was squeezed between two huge trucks and couldn't see around the one in front of me at all. I kept a wary eye on my rearview mirror as the double-trailer gravel truck behind me kept pressing in too close. Suddenly, the gravel truck roared into the oncoming lane. The empty truck bounced, rattled, and rumbled as it thundered past my car and the truck in front of me. In that heart-stopping moment I thought sure we'd have a horrendous accident.

The night was so black I couldn't see to pass the truck or much of anything else on either side of the highway. The only assurance I had was an occasional fluorescent orange detour sign with an arrow pointing the direction I was moving. Otherwise, I felt lost.

When I reached a junction, I saw a patrol car sitting by the road. We were being routed to another highway. For a second I thought about asking the patrolman for directions to a road that would take me directly to Santa Maria. I knew it was close by, but I had no idea how to find it. The truck was still in front of me, however, and instead of stopping, I kept following like a sheep that has no idea where it is being led.

I hadn't been on the second highway very long before I realized we were doubling back in the direction we had come. If I had stopped to ask for help, I would have been home in twenty minutes; now it was going to be a fifty-minute drive.

By now the darkness was dense and blacker than ever. I was overly exhausted and in desperate need of a rest break. Finally, I reached the town of Buellton. I was grateful to see lights, but all the places where I could stop were closed. I quickly found the Highway 101 off-ramp and made it safely home.

After that trip, I thought about the "if onlys." If only I'd listened to my husband and waited to drive home the next morning. If only I'd listened to the quiet nudging of the Holy Spirit to take a break. He knew about the detours and that I'd need rest and relief. Perhaps avoiding the stress would have saved me from the bladder infection that afflicted me afterward.

Wondering about the if onlys cannot change what happened that night. Even so, I gained some insights from that experience. I realized that our lives are similar to those detours that send us on a roundabout way to our destination. It's the uncertainties we feel during those major life detours that try our faith and test our willingness to follow God's ways. If we desire to remain faithful in our spiritual commitment, we need to recognize the following uncertainties of life.

Life's Detours

Life surprises us with unexpected detours. Some are brief inconveniences. Others are dark, long, and terrible. We may never return to the main highway again. Death of a loved one. Divorce. Terminal illness. Loss of a job. The list of major life detours are endless.

If we're going to lead a holy life, we need to be spiritually prepared for detours. It's those unexpected deviations that plunge us into the dark night of the soul and cause us to question our faith. Life may seem leaden black. We may feel lost on an unfamiliar road with hairpin curves and heart-stopping dangers.

While I was writing this book, I had a month off from teaching to devote to the project. But I came down with a severe infection and a week later had the flu. My husband was fighting the same flu and also diabetic reactions. Plus we had a long list of other serious concerns and normal responsibilities.

With my energy depleted from being sick, I could hardly concentrate as I tried to write. I made little progress. My emotions hit a new low, and I wanted to give up. How could I do what I had thought God wanted? It seemed as if He were working against His own plans for my life. Certainly, He was sifting me in the very areas I was writing about. I felt spiritually chastised and challenged.

Once a week my friend Judie and I pray together. One morning when we met during that siege, I started to pray, but I couldn't go on. Instead of words came tears. I had no reserves left. Judie held us both up before the Lord.

Our time of sharing and prayer gave me the courage and support I needed. She had suddenly found herself out of work and needed direction finding another job. I realized I was not alone; we were both facing many hard detours and faith-challenging experiences.

I have come to realize that detours are not just irritating interruptions that prevent us from directly reaching our destination. They may be a well-planned part of our spiritual journey. God often desires to guide us in a way that we would never choose. We want to drive on the straight, easy road that takes us directly home.

God may send us on a circuitous route, because He has a divine appointment or essential spiritual lessons for us and others. Even our darkest detours may be used by the Lord for the sake of encouraging others who find themselves lost on a similar road.

The pressure, stress, and even sorrow related to unexpected detours are meant to draw us closer to the Lord. He is able to redeem for His own glory the most disappointing heartaches and terrible trials. Do we only see those trials as an embittering experience or can we consider them an opportunity for the Lord to demonstrate Himself in a gracious way? Until our faith is made real during a detour on a dark road, we will only see God as the means of satisfying our own needs and serving our own purposes.

Life's Changes

Life constantly changes. God "changes times and seasons; he sets up kings and deposes them" (Dan. 2:21a). Changes range from being a blessing, hardly making a difference, to becoming a sudden tragedy. Our whole life can be changed in a second.

Some changes are not of our own choosing; others we make ourselves. My husband, Ron, and I made major changes recently. We moved from Garden Grove to Santa Maria and changed jobs. I was hired to start new vocational English as a second language classes at our local community college. Ron chose to leave the security of a company he'd worked at for almost twenty-three years.

Though these changes were positive, they were far more difficult than we had anticipated. They have been faith-challenging as we faced many insecurities and unexpected trials.

One of our greatest temptations is to stop walking with the Lord when our circumstances and/or relationships change for the worse. When painful changes shatter our lives, our security is not at stake, but the life of Christ in us.

If we're going to lead godly lives, we need to be spiritually prepared for the sudden and difficult disruptions that come unbidden into our lives. We need to look at them and ask: "Lord, what are You trying to say to me through this painful experience?" "What do You desire to teach me?" "How do You want to use this in my life to glorify You and minister to others?"

Will we allow the Holy Spirit to make Christ real in us no matter how trying the changes? Will He be able to manifest His presence in our lives so that others see Jesus in us?

What happens to us is not for our sake alone, but for the sake of Christ and others. Certainly, God is refining us, and so what happens is for our sake, too. But the Lord always wants to take us beyond ourselves. He has far more to accomplish. He desires to reveal Himself through our greatest heartaches as we demonstrate to others our reliance on Him.

I have come to realize that though our lives may change in ways we could never have imagined, the Lord is steadfast and unmovable. He is our refuge, source of strength, and ever-present help through the fluctuations of life.

Life's Uncertainties

Life is uncertain. "Do not boast about tomorrow, for you do not know what a day may bring forth" (Prov. 27:1). Paul wrote, "And now, compelled by the Spirit, I am going to Jerusalem, not knowing what will happen to me there" (Acts 20:22).

When we moved, I was excited but uncertain about starting new vocational classes at the college. I had not done that before. My previous teaching job was also far more secure. My schedule at the new job varies from semester to semester, because my class assignments constantly change and student enrollment is highly unpredictable.

Ron thought he had work before we first moved to Santa Maria, but all his options fell through while we were moving. We were apprehensive, but he found a position the first week he was here.

Then he lost that job due to a change in company ownership. We wondered if we would be able to stay in Santa Maria, where jobs are scarce and salaries are low. After a month he found work. But then the new company he's working for announced they were selling out.

Shortly after finding that out, we lost our medical insurance. We soon discovered that individual medical premiums were astronomical and unaffordable. My fear level went off the charts.

The following morning as I started to read the day's selection in the *One Year Bible*, I felt prompted to read the psalm from the day before, which said: "I am still confident of this: I will see the goodness of the Lord in the land of the living. Wait for the Lord; be strong and take heart and wait for the Lord" (Ps. 27:13-14).

The next day as I was eating breakfast, I drew a card from our promise box of verses. It was the same passage. God's gracious reassurance gave me the peace to accept the uncertainties we faced.

I realize on a spiritual level that life's uncertainties challenge the validity of my confidence in God. As I persevere by faith, my trust in the Lord will be strengthened. I know in my mind that God is faithful and reliable, but I waver emotionally. I would rather not go through the wrenching process of the trying of my faith. I'd like to be a spiritual superperson, but I'm not. And I suspect I'm not alone.

God has been faithful to us, but the stress of the unknown, anxiety over uncertainties, and the frustrations of waiting for answers is wearying. If we expect to have a secure, stable life without heartaches, then we will be disappointed in the Lord every time. Our faith would be in our expectations and not in God Himself. Faith is certainty in God—not in the answers we desire or the outcome we have decided upon.

If we're going to be godly people of steadfast faith, we need to realize that life can be painfully uncertain. We may have an ideal and unrealistic belief about how God should change the uncertainties we're facing. God, however, desires to transform our faith from shallow belief and self-centered preoccupation into an abiding, unshakable confidence in Him. The certainty of our faith becomes real when it's tested by life's uncertainties.[1]

Life's Unknowns

Our future here on earth is unknown. "A man cannot discover anything about his future" (Eccl. 7:14b). "Now listen, you who say, 'Today or tomorrow we will go to this or that city, spend a year there, carry on business and make money.' Why, you do not even know what will happen tomorrow" (James 4:13-14a).

Looking back over my life, I would never have predicted what has happened to Ron and me—both the good and the bad. I don't have a clear view of our future. But because I have a strong need for security, I've felt anxious and even fearful about the future. Often what I feared did not happen, and I wasted emotional energy worrying.

Jesus said, "Therefore do not worry about tomorrow, for tomorrow will worry about itself. Each day has enough trouble of its own" (Matt. 6:34). I wish it were as easy as that. Some days I have no difficulty trusting the Lord with the future; other days I am overwhelmed with concern. Then I'm ashamed that I worried instead of leaving my problems with the Lord.

We'll grow in godliness as we keep putting our complete trust in the One who knows our future. He desires that we have peace about tomorrow, for He *is* our future and will take care of all our tomorrows.

In the following poem, Judie Frank identifies what so many of us experience as we wrestle with the challenges of unexpected detours, constant changes, uncertainties of life, and our unknown future.

TAKE THEM BACK

I give my problems to the Lord, and then I take them back.
It's not that I don't trust Him or faith that I lack.
It's just I give them to the Lord, and then I take them back.
I'm so sure that I've given all my problems unto Him;
Then all at once I realize I'm burdened down again.
I don't understand the reason I've taken them all back.
So, Lord, I bring them unto You again; please take them back.[2]

Scripture Reading: 1 Samuel 20:27-42; 22:1-5; 23:7-18

Practicing the Spiritual Life

How did David seek help during the many difficult detours he had to take?

If you are experiencing unexpected detours, how do you feel about them, and what steps will you take to seek the Lord's direction?

Prayer

Ever-watchful God, "if I go up to the heavens, you are there; if I make my bed in the depths, you are there. If I rise on the wings of the dawn, if I settle on the far side of the sea, even there your hand will guide me, your right hand will hold me fast." You will lead me when I cannot see, by ways I have not known, along unfamiliar paths You will guide me; You will turn the darkness into light before me and make the rough places smooth. These are the things You will do; You will not forsake me. (Ps. 139:8-10 not paraphrased; Isa. 42:16 paraphrased)

Prayers, Praises, and Personal Notes

Scripture Reading: 1 Samuel 25:2-35

Practicing the Spiritual Life

What changes and possible losses did Abigail face? What did she wisely do and say to prevent them from happening?

_____

_____

_____

What difficult changes are you experiencing? What wisdom can you gain from the way Abigail dealt with her problem?

_____

_____

_____

Prayer

All-wise God, as I go through these difficult changes in my life, may I have an understanding heart that seeks knowledge, and not the mouth of a fool that feeds on foolishness and folly. May I be a person of wisdom who hears and increases my learning, and a person of understanding who attains wise counsel. May I trust in You, Lord, and do good; then I will dwell in the land and enjoy safe pasture. And this is my prayer: that my love may abound more and more in knowledge and depth of insight, so that I may be able to discern what is best. (Prov. 15:14 KJV; 1:5 KJV; Ps. 37:3; Phil. 1:9-10a paraphrased)

Prayers, Praises, and Personal Notes

_____

_____

_____

_____

Scripture Reading: 1 Kings 17:1-24

Practicing the Spiritual Life

What uncertainties did the widow face? How was her faith challenged? What unexpected and heartbreaking changes did she experience?

_____

_____

_____

What encouragement do you find in this story for the faith-challenging uncertainties that you may be experiencing?

_____

_____

_____

Prayer

O Lord, I am facing so many uncertainties. For You have blocked my way so I cannot pass; You have shrouded my paths in darkness. You have made my heart faint; Almighty God, You have terrified me. "When I looked for good, then evil came to me; when I waited for light, there came darkness." "Forsake me not, O Lord; O my God, be not far from me." Be my strength for I am poor; be my refuge and strength, for I am needy in my distress; be my shelter from the storm and a shade from the heat. I am casting my burdens on You, Lord, and releasing the weight of them to You, for You will sustain me. (Job 19:8; 23:16 paraphrased; Job 30:26 AMP; Ps. 38:21 AMP not paraphrased; Isa. 25:4a KJV; Ps. 55:22a AMP paraphrased)

Prayers, Praises, and Personal Notes

_____

_____

_____

Scripture Reading: Esther 3:12–4:17; 7:1-10; 9:1-5

Practicing the Spiritual Life

How did Esther handle her uncertain fate and that of the Jewish people?

Are you grieving about any changes or uncertainties in your life? If so, what would bring you comfort?

Prayer

"When I am afraid, I will trust in you." Though I am uncertain about what will happen, You, Lord, will go before me and will be with me; You will never leave me nor forsake me. Therefore, I will not be afraid; I will not be discouraged. I will be strong and courageous. I will trust in You at all times; I will pour out my heart to You, for You are my refuge. "I eagerly expect and hope that I will in no way be ashamed, but will have sufficient courage so that now as always Christ will be exalted in my body, whether by life or by death." (Ps. 56:3 not paraphrased; Deut. 31:8, 6a; Ps. 62:8 paraphrased; Phil. 1:20 not paraphrased)

Prayers, Praises, and Personal Notes

Scripture Reading: Luke 1:26-55

Practicing the Spiritual Life

We may experience wonderful changes in our lives that we can celebrate. How did Mary respond to the surprising announcement that changed her life forever?

_____

_____

_____

List some of the blessings that have changed your life and that you have celebrated in the past and/or present.

_____

_____

_____

Prayer

"I will praise you, O Lord my God, with all my heart; I will glorify your name forever." "Your righteousness reaches to the skies, O God, you who have done great things. Who, O God, is like you?" How great are Your signs, how mighty Your wonders! Your kingdom is an eternal kingdom; Your dominion endures from generation to generation. "I will meditate on all your works and consider all your mighty deeds." Lord, You have done great things for me, and I am filled with joy. (Ps. 86:12; Ps. 71:19 not paraphrased; Dan. 4:3 paraphrased; Ps. 77:12 not paraphrased; Ps. 126:3 paraphrased)

Prayers, Praises, and Personal Notes

_____

_____

_____

Scripture Reading: Matthew 28:1-10

Practicing the Spiritual Life

When Mary and Mary Magdalene went to Jesus' tomb, they were uncertain about His fate. How did the women feel after seeing the angel?

_____

_____

_____

Describe how you felt if you have ever heard good news after being uncertain about the outcome of a difficult trial.

_____

_____

_____

Prayer

Jesus, I am filled with an inexpressible and glorious joy. For I believe You died and rose again, so I am certain that God will bring with You those who have fallen asleep having faith in You. For Lord, You Yourself will come down from heaven with a loud command, with the voice of the archangel and with the trumpet call of God, and the dead who are believers will rise first. After that, if I am still alive and left, I will be caught up together with them in the clouds to meet You, Lord, in the air. And so I will be with You forever. (1 Peter 1:8b; 1 Thess. 4:14, 16, 17 paraphrased)

Prayers, Praises, and Personal Notes

_____

_____

_____

_____

Scripture Reading: Luke 12:13-21

Practicing the Spiritual Life

What should the rich man have considered before making decisions about his unknown future?

_____

_____

_____

Ask the Lord to show you how He would desire you to prepare for the future.

_____

_____

_____

Prayer

O God, I will not fret because of evil people or be envious of the wicked, for the evil person has no future hope. Therefore, I will not let my heart envy sinners, but will always be zealous for the fear of You. I know also that wisdom is sweet to my soul; if I find it, there is a future hope for me. Yet I do not know the future, and no person can tell me what is to come. I do not have power over the wind to contain it; so I do not have power over the day of my death. Still there is surely a future hope for me, because I know that the One who raised You, Lord Jesus, from the dead will also raise me with You. (Prov. 24:19-20a; 23:17; 24:14a; Eccl. 8:7-8a; Prov. 23:18a; 2 Cor. 4:14a paraphrased)

Prayers, Praises, and Personal Notes

_____

_____

_____

WEEK SIX

Relinquish Your Heart's Desires

"During the days of Jesus' life on earth, he offered up prayers and petitions with loud cries and tears to the one who could save him from death, and he was heard because of his reverent submission."

HEBREWS 5:7

*H*old my hand," said Katelyn.

My two-year old granddaughter, her brother Byron, and I were at the pond in the park. Katelyn loves to feed the ducks and geese, but their honking, quacking, and squabbling scared her. She felt safe as long as she could hold my hand and stay beside me while she watched them gobble up puffy white kernels of popcorn.

Another time we had an electrical blackout when I was watching Katelyn for a few hours. By evening it was black outside and inside the house. She didn't seem to be scared of the darkness. She played with a flashlight, turning it off and on and shining it in her face. We even read an animal picture book by flashlight.

I put her to bed at eight-thirty and lay on the bed beside her. She didn't say a word, but she reached out to find my hand.

She tossed and turned restlessly trying to fall asleep but never let go of my hand. Every time I released her hand to see if she had fallen asleep, she would reach out in the dark until she found mine. When I thought she had fallen asleep, I got up.

I dressed for bed, and then I heard her call me in her small quiet voice, "GrandMary."

"Would you like apple juice or milk?" I asked.

"Juicy," she answered.

I got her a bottle of juice and laid back down beside her. She drank her bottle with one hand and held mine with her other hand until she finally fell asleep.

An Unseen Hand

Just as Katelyn felt secure and her fears were eased when she held my hand, so we need the sense of God's unseen hand holding ours. We need that comfort when we experience frightening trials. Recently I felt panic at receiving bad news from Ron's doctor while we faced the impending loss of medical insurance and the possible loss of his job.

Also one of our family members works as a night custodian at an elementary school in a gang-infested area. He's had to make almost nightly police calls because of drug dealings and gang activities. Despite repeated requests for protective fencing and gates, these haven't been installed.

Frankly, I felt nearly paralyzed with concern. As I opened Oswald Chambers's book, *My Utmost for His Highest*, I randomly turned to a devotional titled "The Never-Failing God." "For he hath said, I will never leave thee, nor forsake thee. So that we may boldly say, The Lord is my helper, and I will not fear what man shall do unto me" (Heb. 13:5b-6 KJV).

"Have I really let God say to me that He will never fail me? If I have listened to this say-so of God's, then let me listen again."[1]

Here I was needing to listen again and again. Then I read the next day's devotional, which said, "God says—'I will never leave thee,' then I can with good courage say—'The Lord is my helper, I will not fear'—I will not be haunted by apprehension. This does not mean that I will not be tempted to fear, but I will remember God's say-so. . . . Faith in many a one falters when the apprehensions come; they forget the meaning of God's say-so, forget to take a deep breath spiritually. The only way to get the dread taken out of us is to listen to God's say-so."[2]

I realized I was filled with apprehension, dread, and panic and did not have the slightest confidence in God. As I pondered those devotionals and prayed, I began to release my fears to the Lord. I took His unseen hand, and peace returned. Fortunately, about a month later we learned that Ron was going to keep his job after all.

The Prayer of Relinquishment

Many years ago I read Catherine Marshall's book *Beyond Ourselves*, and her chapter, "The Prayer of Relinquishment" had a profound effect on my spiritual growth, strengthened my relationship with the Lord, and helped me maintain my faith.

Throughout the years, I have prayed the Prayer of Relinquishment and released many trials and heartaches to God. Now here I was again needing to let go of my fears about our future, needing to relinquish the health and safety of my loved ones to the Lord, needing to reach out for God's strong hand by faith.

To lead a holy life, we need to realize that relinquishment is essential to the building and strengthening of our faith. If Satan would weaken our confidence in the Lord, it is almost always in the area of our heart's greatest needs and desires. We are most vulnerable to spiritual defeat and wavering trust when those longings go unmet.

Why is the Prayer of Relinquishment essential to our spiritual maturity and well-being? Through it we become focused on God's will and desires. We open ourselves to seeing how God will answer in His own way. Catherine Marshall said, "If relinquishment is real, the one praying must be willing to receive or not receive his heart's desire."[3]

Relinquishment is more than prayer; it is an act of surrender. This means we give over the possession and control of our desires and needs to God. We leave them behind, let them go, and stop holding onto them emotionally, mentally, physically, and spiritually.

We not only put our desires aside, but we completely release them to the Lord and even renounce them. We refuse to allow obsessive thoughts about what we desperately need, recognizing that we may need to seek pastoral or professional help if we find ourselves unable to stop these thoughts.

The greatest sorrow may come when we lose someone we love or an important material possession. It's difficult enough when we make the choice to let go, but when we're stripped of what we hold dear, the relinquishment process may be excruciatingly painful.

If we're going to remain spiritually strong, we need to be prepared to release our heartfelt needs to the Lord. Our desires may not be sinful; they may be holy. We may be praying for people to find salvation or recommit their lives to the Lord. We have legitimate needs. Nonetheless, we may have to relinquish all those requests and desires to the Lord as well as our ambitions, goals, and plans; lack of health, justice, and material goods; imperfect life, personal rights, and—most of all—people.

Relinquishment, however, is not resignation, nor does it mean that we stop praying. "Resignation is barren of faith in the love of God. It says, 'Grievous circumstances have come to me. There is no escaping them. . . . So I'll just resign myself to what apparently is the will of God; I'll even try to make a virtue out of patient submission.' So resignation lies down quietly in the dust of a universe from which God seems to have fled, and the door of Hope swings shut."[4]

On the contrary, relinquishment doesn't weaken our hope; it strengthens our confidence in the Lord. False hope and faith believe that He will meet our needs according to our specifications. Genuine faith is placed entirely in the Lord and not in how He may answer. "Thus faith is by no means absent in the Prayer of Relinquishment. In fact this prayer is faith in action. . . . And the act of placing what we cherish most in His hands is to Him the sweet music of the essence of faith."[5]

Hindrances to Relinquishment

What hindrances do we experience in our faith when we're unable to relinquish our desires to the Lord? We become more focused on ourselves. We presume upon God to answer our prayers in a narrow, prescribed way. We dictate to God exactly what He should do. Then when He doesn't answer as we determined or takes too long, we're disappointed.

On the other hand, we may deny reality and pretend that we don't have any heartaches and unmet desires. We may give the impression that all is well when behind this spiritual facade, our lives are actually falling to pieces. Or we may claim that God is going to do a miracle. We may convince ourselves that He will quickly grant us the answers we hope for.

"That hope, however, is a lie, an appealing but grotesque perversion of the good news of Christ. It's a lie responsible for leading hundreds of thousands of seeking people into either a powerless lifestyle of denial and fabricated joy or turning away from Christianity in disillusionment and disgust. It's a lie that blocks the path to the deep transformation of character that *is* available now. . . . But to demand that our groaning end before Heaven keeps us from all that's available now."[6]

We want our pain to be over now, but it is through those very trials that our trust in the Lord is tested. When our lives are shattered, it is for the purpose of purifying our faith. We discover whether it is genuine and how willing we are to lead a holy life. God's purpose for our lives is the transformation of our character.

We need to be transparent before the Lord about our heartaches. We need to allow ourselves to grieve. Then we are more able to realistically work through our pain. We may need to deal with anger, anxiety, and depression. We may be bitter and accuse God of failing us as the heavens seem to remain silent and nothing changes. It's essential that we realize that this is part of the process of working through our grief, but if we lock ourselves into those darker places, we will not be able to complete the relinquishment process.

Do we desire to be holy, or do we desire to be blessed? Is our motive for following God's ways set on the answers we expect to receive? Is our commitment to Christ based on having good feelings, good times, and good health?[7]

As long as we want Him to serve our own purposes, He is not Lord of our life. If we relinquish our desires and needs to Him, we are prepared for Him to do whatever He pleases. Until we do, we'll be bound by our fears as we anxiously wait for answers.

"What is this spiritual law implicit in this Prayer of Relinquishment? . . . We know that fear blocks prayer. Fear is a barrier erected between us and God, so that his power cannot get through to us. So—how does one get rid of fear?"[8]

"This is not easy when the life of someone dear hangs in the balance, or when what we want most in all the world seems to be slipping away. At such times every emotion, every passion, is tied up in the dread that what we fear most is about to come upon us. Obviously only strong measures can deal with such a powerful fear."[9]

The Process of Relinquishment

When we feel as if we have no emotional, physical, or spiritual reserves left to cope, we need to humble ourselves before the Lord and admit the power of our fears and weakness. Who more than David poured out his fright before the Lord without shame. "Fear and trembling have beset me; horror has overwhelmed me" (Ps. 55:5).

I've found that I need to work through this process in order to release my concerns and be relieved of my all-consuming fears. Confessing to and praying with a prayer partner, and relying on the Word of God to speak to my needs has helped me the most. I also write out my concerns and the Scriptures that speak to these and minister to my heart.

I cling to the promises of God, such as, "For I am the Lord, your God, who takes hold of your right hand and says to you, Do not fear; I will help you" (Isa. 41:13). Sometimes I open my hands and hold them out to the Lord, or I lay on the floor facedown with my hands stretched out as an act of relinquishment.

I may repeat a paraphrased Scripture prayer, such as: *I will not fear, for*

You are with me: I will not be dismayed, for You are my God. You will strengthen me; yes, You will help me; yes, You will uphold me with the right hand of Your righteousness. (Isa. 41:10 KJV).

Acceptance is the next important key to relinquishment. "Acceptance says, 'I trust the good will, the love of my God. I'll open my arms and my understanding to what He has allowed to come to me. Since I know that He means to make all things work together for good, I consent to this present situation with hope for what the future will bring.' Thus acceptance leaves the door of Hope wide open to God's creative plan."[10]

The final step in relinquishment comes when the Lord's desires become our desires. "Delight yourself in the Lord and he will give you the desires of your heart. Commit your way to the Lord; trust in him and he will do this" (Ps. 37:4-5). How often we focus on "He will give you the desires of your heart." We put all our hopes in our own desires and think only of how desperately we want God to grant them.

When we do, we don't see the conditions vital to having the desires of our heart met. As we delight in the Lord, we express our gratitude to Him for who He is and what He means to us apart from what we desire. As we commit our way to the Lord, we are letting go of *our* desires so that *His* desires may become ours. Then as we trust completely in Him, He will grant us the desires of our heart—because now our desires and His are the same.

Scripture Reading: Matthew 26:36-45

Practicing the Spiritual Life

When Jesus offered His prayer of relinquishment to His Father, what did He surrender, and how did He feel about it?

_____

_____

_____

If you're in sorrow and troubled about a need that God wants you to relinquish to Him, express your feelings to Him.

_____

_____

_____

Prayer

Jesus, I will keep awake and watch and pray constantly that I may not enter into temptation; my spirit indeed is willing, but my flesh is weak. "I confess my sins; I am deeply sorry for what I have done." "How long must I struggle with anguish in my soul, with sorrow in my heart every day?" "My grief is beyond healing; my heart is broken." "Have mercy on me, Lord, for I am in distress. My sight is blurred because of my tears. My body and soul are withering away." "I have great sorrow and unceasing anguish in my heart." "I weep with grief; encourage me by your word." (Mark 14:38 AMP paraphrased; Ps. 38:18 NLT; 13:2a NLT; Jer. 8:18 NLT; Ps. 31:9 NLT; Rom. 9:2; Ps. 119:28 NLT not paraphrased)

Prayers, Praises, and Personal Notes

_____

_____

_____

Scripture Reading: Luke 23:32-46

Practicing the Spiritual Life

What did Jesus suffer on the cross as He relinquished His life? What did Jesus pray for those who crucified Him?

_____

_____

_____

Do you need to work through the process of relinquishment regarding a certain desire? Is there anyone you need to forgive? Write a prayer for this process.

_____

_____

_____

Prayer

During the days of Your life on earth, Jesus, You offered up prayers and petitions with loud cries and tears to the One who could save You from death, and You were heard because of Your reverent submission. Therefore, You are able to save me completely as I come to You, Jesus, because You always live to intercede for me. And now as I am praying, I will not hold anything against any person; I forgive, so that You, Father in heaven, may forgive me of my sins. Into Your hand I commit my spirit and relinquish my life to You; for You have redeemed me. (Heb. 5:7; 7:25; Mark 11:25; Ps. 31:5 KJV paraphrased)

Prayers, Praises, and Personal Notes

_____

_____

_____

Scripture Reading: John 19:23-27

Practicing the Spiritual Life

What was taken from Jesus that He had no choice about? Whom did He relinquish to the care of the apostle John?

_____

_____

_____

Has someone or something you cherished been taken from you that you need to relinquish to the Lord? If so, ask the Lord to show you how to begin the process of letting go.

_____

_____

_____

Prayer

Arise, Lord! Lift up your hand, O God. Do not forget me as I am helpless. You, O God, see my trouble and grief; You consider it to take it in hand. I commit myself to You, for You are my helper. Show the wonder of Your great love to me, You who save me by Your right hand, for I take refuge in You from my foes. Lord, You stand at my right hand when I am needy, to save my life from those who condemn me. You hear my desires when I am afflicted; You encourage me and listen to my cry. (Ps. 10:12, 14; 17:7; 109:31; 10:17 paraphrased)

Prayers, Praises, and Personal Notes

_____

_____

_____

Scripture Reading: Philemon

Practicing the Spiritual Life

Where was Paul, and how did he use that experience as an appeal to Philemon to release Onesimus? How did Paul feel about relinquishing Onesimus to Philemon?

_____

_____

_____

What specific steps will you take to work through the process of relinquishment?

_____

_____

_____

Prayer

Lord, I relinquish those I love and care about into your hands. Search them, O God, and know their hearts; try them, and know their thoughts. And see if there be any wicked way in them, and lead them in the way everlasting. In the time of Your favor answer them, and in the day of salvation help them and keep them. Say to those who are captives, "Come out," and to those in darkness, "Be free!" O Shepherd of their souls, have compassion on them, guide them, and lead them beside springs of living water. (Ps. 139:23-24 KJV; Isa. 49:8a, 9a, 10b paraphrased)

Prayers, Praises, and Personal Notes

_____

_____

_____

Scripture Reading: Hebrews 10:32-39

Practicing the Spiritual Life
How were believers treated, and what was taken from them? What was their attitude about what they suffered and their losses?

_____

_____

_____

Are you suffering insults or persecution? Is there any area of your life where you need to persevere by faith and not shrink back?

_____

_____

_____

Prayer
Ever-forgiving Savior, You said this to me, and I hear You: I will love my enemies, do good to them that hate me, bless them that curse me, and pray for them that despitefully use me. And to those that strike me on the one cheek, I will offer also the other; and those that take away my cloak, I will forbid them not to take my coat also. I will give to everyone who asks of me; and of them that take away my goods, I will ask for them not again. I will love my enemies and do good and lend, hoping for nothing again; and my reward shall be great, and I shall be Your child, O most High, for I will be kind to the unthankful and to the evil. (Luke 6:27-30, 35 KJV paraphrased)

Prayers, Praises, and Personal Notes

_____

_____

_____

Scripture Reading: Hebrews 11:8-10

Practicing the Spiritual Life

How did Abraham, Isaac, and Jacob live? What did they relinquish by doing so? What did they look forward to by faith?

_____

_____

_____

Though relinquishment may be difficult, we also need to look forward and hold on to what God has promised us. Find promises in the Word to help you through this process and to strengthen your faith. Write the verses here.

_____

_____

_____

Prayer

Heavenly Father, I am an alien and stranger before You, and a sojourner, as were all my forbears. For here I do not have an enduring city, but I am looking for the city that is to come. Therefore, I live by faith, not by sight. Now faith is being sure of what I hope for and certain of what I do not see. And without faith it is impossible to please You, God, because when I come to You, I must believe that You exist and that You reward me for earnestly seeking You. (1 Chron. 29:15a KJV; Heb. 13:14; 2 Cor. 5:7; Heb. 11:1, 6 paraphrased)

Prayers, Praises, and Personal Notes

_____

_____

_____

Scripture Reading: Hebrews 11:11-19

Practicing the Spiritual Life

What did the people of God receive in place of what they relinquished? How was Abraham's willingness to relinquish his son tested?

_____

_____

_____

Do you feel as if your willingness to relinquish is being tested? What do you hope to receive in place of what you give up?

_____

_____

_____

Prayer

Father God, "Against all hope, Abraham in hope believed and so became the father of many nations." Yet he did not waver through unbelief regarding Your promise, God, but was strengthened in his faith and gave glory to You, being fully persuaded that You had power to do what You had promised. "This is why 'it was credited to him as righteousness.'" The words "it was credited to him" were written not for him alone, but for me also; You will credit me with righteousness—for I believe in You who raised Jesus my Lord from the dead. (Rom. 4:18a not paraphrased; Rom. 4:20-21 paraphrased; Rom. 4:22 not paraphrased; Rom. 4:23-24 paraphrased)

Prayers, Praises, and Personal Notes

_____

_____

_____

_____

WEEK SEVEN

Release Your Life to God

"I thank Christ Jesus our Lord,
who has given me strength,
that he considered me faithful,
appointing me to his service."

1 TIMOTHY 1:12

During World War II, Corrie ten Boom and her family concealed Dutch and Jewish people in their home and helped them escape to freedom. After a traitor turned the ten Booms in, they were arrested and incarcerated in a prison in Holland.

In her cell Corrie often prayed, "Lord, never let the enemy put me in a German concentration camp."[1]

But when Corrie was in her fifties and her sister Betsie, fifty-nine, they were shipped in a railroad boxcar to the Ravensbruck concentration camp in Germany. There they experienced the atrocities of evil. More than 96,000 women died in that prison.

Yet in that torturous camp, Corrie and Betsie held clandestine Bible studies twice a day. Many women who had never heard of Jesus came to know Him as their Savior. Corrie said, "If God had not used my sister Betsie and me to bring them to Him, they would never have heard of Him. Many died with the name of Jesus on their lips. They were well worth all our suffering."[2]

The week after Betsie died in the concentration camp, Corrie was standing with the ranks of women prisoners during roll call. When her number and name were called and she was told to stand on the number one, Corrie wondered what it meant. The prisoners were never called by name.

As she stood in the freezing weather in her ragged prison dress, she wondered if she would soon join her sister in heaven. She thought it would be her last chance to witness for Christ, and so she began sharing the Gospel with Tiny, the girl standing next to her, who had never read the Bible.

Other prisoners nearby listened as Corrie told them how her sister had just died and that Jesus was always with them no matter how much they had suffered. He had even freed Corrie from hating her enemies, though her father, sister, and other family members had died in prison or the death camps.

As they stood for nearly three hours, Corrie continued telling Tiny about Jesus, and the girl accepted the Lord. That very morning Tiny died, but by a divine "clerical mistake," Corrie was released from Ravensbruck.

Releasing Our Lives to the Lord

During our jouney toward holiness, we need to keep releasing our lives to God. Corrie experienced the depth of what it means to relinquish her life to serve the Lord. She had lost in the very bowels of hell all she held dear—her family, friends, freedom, basic comforts of home, safety, and security. She had experienced starvation, torture, and the deepest suffering of her life.

Corrie wanted to return to her town, to the home she had lived in for fifty-three years, and to her profession as a watchmaker. But she surrendered her life to God and became a "tramp" for the Lord.

During the later years of life when many retire, Corrie shared the Gospel and her testimony in more than sixty countries. Corrie spoke to thousands of people in many different situations from the darkest prisons to the grandest churches.

She traveled around the world twice and slept in more than a thousand beds; some were comfortable, others straw mats on dirt floors. She lived and ministered as Jesus did without a place that she could call her own. She gave up the security of having a home and the peace of sleeping in her own bed to become dependent upon the hospitality of strangers for food, lodging, and financial support.

At seventy-three years of age, she was so exhausted and ill, she wanted to give up her extensive speaking schedule. She decided she would stop traveling and make a home in Africa, but then an African Christian told her about how her words had ministered to him in prison.

Then he read her a passage from Revelation, "Repent and live as you lived at first. Otherwise, if your heart remains unchanged, I shall come to you and remove your lamp stand from its place" (Rev. 1:5 PHILLIPS).

She felt convicted. "I had lost my first love," she realized. "Twenty years before I had come out of a concentration camp—starved, weak—but in my heart there was a burning love: a love for the Lord who had carried me through so faithfully—a love for the people around me—a burning desire to tell them that Jesus is a reality, that He lives, that He is Victor. . . . I wanted everyone to know that no matter how deep we fall, the Everlasting Arms are always under us to carry us out."[3]

Corrie asked the Lord for forgiveness, surrendered her "cold heart," and returned to her calling as a tramp for the Lord. She continued her journeys until she was eighty-five years old. On February 28, 1944, Corrie had gone to prison. Exactly thirty-three years later on February 28, 1977, she moved into her own home. Though she stopped traveling, she kept up her world-wide ministry.[4]

God Teaches Us His Way

After experiencing the depth of such cruelty and loss in the concentration camp, you would think that life might have been easier for Corrie. But she continued to endure hardships and learned many more lessons in releasing her life to the Lord as she traveled around the world.

She wrote, "When I left the German concentration camp, I said, 'I'll go anywhere God sends me, but I hope never to Germany.' Now I understand that was a statement of disobedience. F. B. Meyer said, 'God does not fill with His Holy Spirit those who believe in the fullness of the Spirit, or those who desire Him, but those who obey Him.'"[5]

Corrie did return to Germany, the land of her enemies. With the help of friends she rented a concentration camp and turned it into a home for refugees. They removed the barbed wire. "Flowers, light-colored paint, and God's love in the hearts of the people changed a cruel camp into a refuge where people would find the way back to life again."[6] Many groups and churches assisted in rebuilding the shelter while Corrie raised money for the work during her travels.

Psalm 32:8 had been Corrie's parents' life verse. "I will instruct thee and teach thee in the way which thou shalt go: I will guide thee with mine eye" (KJV). Corrie said, "Now that Father and Mother were gone, this promise became the special directive for my life as well—God's pledge to guide me in all my journeys."[7]

To be holy, we need to release our lives to the Lord so that He may guide and instruct us in the way He desires us to go. The vast majority of us will not be called to serve God in such an extraordinary way as Corrie. Though we may think our lives are ordinary, He desires that we daily yield ourselves to Him so we may serve Him. The Lord has many divine appointments for us to share the Gospel and to minister to family, friends, and strangers.

As we release our lives to God, He will use us in ways we cannot imagine. He will allow us to go through many experiences that are not meant for us alone. Everything that happens to us is not just for or about us; it's about what God desires to do through us.

For example, God used Norma in my life in a special way. I rarely went to church as a child, but when I was sixteen, Norma invited me to her church. One evening she shared how to become a Christian. It was the first time I remember hearing the Gospel. Shortly afterward I accepted Christ when I was alone in my bedroom.

After being out of touch with her for many years, one day I received a call from Norma. She was surprised when I shared with her that it was through her witness that I had become a Christian.

When we release ourselves to the Lord, He will use us in ways we may not realize. God simply used Norma to lead me to the Lord, and that decision changed my entire life.

The Best Remains

When Corrie was in her eighties, she talked to a group of students in the Midwest. She said, "I told them of the joy of having Jesus with me, whatever happened, and how I knew from experience that the light of Jesus is stronger than the greatest darkness. I told them of the darkness of my prison experiences. . . . I wanted these students to know that even though I was there where every day 600 people either died or were killed, when Jesus is with you, the worst can happen and the best remains."[8]

Our idea of the best remaining is far different from God's. Why was Corrie spared while her family members were killed? Betsie and their father were in a far better place in heaven, but why such cruel deaths? It's a mystery, and only God knows that answer. The best that remained was Corrie's willingness to serve the Lord even though she suffered such unbearable losses.

To lead a holy, purified life, we need to realize that we may suffer as we serve Him. Releasing ourselves to the Lord does not mean we're exempt from terrible and unfair tribulations. The worst can happen, and out of the ashes the best can remain. If we are willing, Christ will redeem our losses and painful prisonlike experiences.

We may even be the ones who make the worst happen by our foolish mistakes, rebelliousness, and sins. If we repent and allow the Lord to do His transforming work in our lives, the best can remain.

Certainly, I have not experienced what Corrie went through, but I have also discovered this principle in my own life. I have given up many things that were good and right and that I dearly loved because God had other plans. I was the director of a preschool and planned to make that my career. Through many different experiences, but mostly by the strong hand of God's pressure,

I left that field to begin a writing ministry. But I wrote with a rebellious attitude. I never had a desire to write and soon discovered that it was extremely difficult.

I paid dearly for that attitude, and so did my family. For five years, I suffered from numerous infections and was on antibiotics for a year. I went through two major surgeries and many other heartaches and difficulties. Though I wrote, I continued to fight against it, even though God kept confirming His will in many amazing ways. Articles and books were published, but I still had not surrendered my will, released my life to the Lord to do whatever He pleased with me.

Gradually I began to have a change of heart. A desire began to grow within me to write about the spiritual life. Instead I edited the work of other authors and wrote a variety of articles and stories. Many of them I put away in cabinets.

I was in constant conflict with myself and had no sense of direction. I felt inadequate and began doubting that I could write anything publishable. My actions were self-defeating, like the fearful children of Israel who didn't trust the Lord to guide them safely into the Promised Land. The greatest fear of my life was that God would become so angry He'd sentence me to wandering in a "desert." My life would be wasted because of my complaining, lack of trust, and rebellious attitude. Finally, I came to the point where I didn't feel I could write anything at all.

About that time, God impressed upon my heart that I should return to college and earn a degree. I didn't want to do that either, but the whole time I was in school, the urgency to finish stayed with me. After graduation, I felt led to teach English as a second language part time.

Then I was hired as a book editor for a Christian publisher, and the desire to have a writing ministry returned. During that time, I met with a woman to seek spiritual counsel. After I told her about my personal conflicts over writing, she asked me, "What if you never write again?"

How could she ask me such a question? What if she's right? I thought.

I felt as if my heart had been pierced. Give up writing? No, I could not accept that. I left our meeting shaken and more determined to write. But I questioned whether God would use me after my rebellion. Where once every fiber of my being had rejected what God desired, now I had a passion to write.

But I was only able to squeeze in a few moments of writing here and there because of my long working hours.

Then the publishing company announced they were moving out of state, and God impressed upon my heart that I should not make that move. I immediately found an excellent part-time teaching position at the college where I had taught before. I needed to work and was grateful for the provision, but I doubted that I'd ever have a writing ministry. Finally, I surrendered my will to the Lord and released my life to Him to do with as He desired.

Though I'd rebelled and did not fully follow the Lord's will for my life, He mercifully redeemed my mistakes. During those long desert years, while I completed college, taught English, and edited books, God was preparing me and teaching me many spiritual lessons.

I came to realize that He had been helping me make changes in my heart's attitude. I had been through many different kinds of experiences both positive and painful that transformed my faith and my life. I learned that in our journey toward holiness, we may often fail, but God restores us as we renew our commitment to do His will.

At it turned out, it was about sixteen years between the publication of my second and third books. During those years, I'd kept a spiritual journal. Through that process God was refining my life and my writing, which became the basis for *A Woman's Walk with God: A Daily Guide for Prayer & Spiritual Growth*. I am deeply thankful that God redeemed my life and that out of the worst the best remained.

Surrender

I have come to realize that God doesn't force us to surrender to Him. He may allow adversity to convict us of our need to submit, but even in trials He does not enforce His way upon us.

Our spirit may be broken. Our health destroyed. Our emotions frayed. Though we may lose loved ones, and every earthly possession of importance may be stripped from us, and we are at the absolute bottom, we are still free to say no to God. We may refuse to submit ourselves and turn away from Him, though we have nothing left and are without hope. We may continue to resist the powerful conviction of the Holy Spirit.

Releasing our lives to God so He may accomplish His will and purposes is our responsibility, not His. He may use circumstances or people to narrow our choices, but we are still free to rebel in our hearts.

To lead a holy life, we are responsible to obey God and submit to His will. When we do, the Holy Spirit will instruct and teach us in the way we should go and by His grace give us the abilities we need to accomplish His desires. "The tiniest detail in which I obey has all the omnipotent power of the grace of God behind it. If I do my duty, not for duty's sake, but because I believe God is engineering my circumstances, then at the very point of my obedience the whole superb grace of God is mine. . . . "[9]

Serve with Love

If we would be holy, love needs to be our highest motivation for obeying and serving the Lord and others. "Whoever has my commands and obeys them, he is the one who loves me" (John 14:21a). "A new command I give you: Love one another. As I have loved you, so you must love one another" (John 13:34).

Being a loving servant is always a challenge when we must minister to difficult people and to those with whom we may have serious personality differences. Corrie ten Boom experienced the highest test, which was to love her enemy. At a church in Berlin, her former prison guard came and asked her for forgiveness. As he stood before her, she felt deeply bitter and recalled the terrible suffering of her dying sister. Corrie knew at that moment that her inability to forgive was more harmful than the whip of the guard.

So she cried, "Lord, thank You for Romans 5:5: 'The love of God is shed abroad in our hearts by the Holy Ghost which is in us.' Thank You, Lord, that Your love in me can do that which I cannot do.

"At that moment a great stream of love poured out of me, and I said, 'Brother, give me your hand. I forgive all. . . .' I could not do it. I was not able. Jesus in me was able to do it. You see, you never touch so much the ocean of God's love as when you love your enemies."[10]

Jesus' love enables us to forgive. When we think we are unable to love, Jesus in us will love others. He will pour His great stream of love through us as we serve each other.

Scripture Reading: Exodus 3:1-15

Practicing the Spiritual Life

When God called Moses to serve Him, how did Moses react? What did God tell Moses about who He is?

Are you fearful of surrendering your will and releasing your life to God for His service because, like Moses, you feel inadequate?

Prayer

Lord, I hear Your voice saying, "Whom shall I send, and who will go for us?" I say, "Here am I; send me." I delight to do Your will, O my God; yes, Your law is within my heart. Have You not commanded me? Be strong and of a good courage; be not afraid, neither be dismayed: for, O Lord my God, You are with me wherever I go. You will be with me; You will not fail me nor forsake me. Therefore, I will be strong and very courageous that I may observe to do according to all the law; I will turn not from it to the right hand or to the left, that I may prosper wherever I go. (Isa. 6:8 KJV; Ps. 40:8 KJV; Josh. 1:9, 5b, 7a, c KJV paraphrased)

Prayers, Praises, and Personal Notes

Scripture Reading: Exodus 3:16–4:18

Practicing the Spiritual Life

Why did Moses feel He was unqualified to serve God? How did God promise to help Moses?

_____

_____

_____

How did God's promise to Moses speak to you about surrendering your life to God no matter how unqualified you may feel?

_____

_____

_____

Prayer

O Counselor and Holy Spirit, sent by the Father in Jesus name, teach me all things. For I am like a deaf person who cannot hear, like a mute who cannot open his mouth; I have become like a person who does not hear, whose mouth can offer no reply. "O Lord, open my lips, and my mouth will declare your praise." Then I will not hide Your righteousness in my heart; I will speak of Your faithfulness and salvation. I will not conceal Your love and Your truth from the great assembly. "My tongue will speak of your righteousness and of your praises all day long." (John 14:26a; Ps. 38:13-14 paraphrased; Ps. 51:15 not paraphrased; Ps. 40:10 paraphrased; Ps. 35:28 not paraphrased)

Prayers, Praises, and Personal Notes

_____

_____

_____

Scripture Reading: John 14:15-31

Practicing the Spiritual Life

What does Jesus promise those who love and obey Him?

_____

_____

_____

In what ways do you need to release your life to the Lord so that you may love and obey Him?

_____

_____

_____

Prayer

Ever-caring Lord, You love those who love You, and those who seek You find You. You show your love to a thousand generations of those who love You and keep Your commandments. I love You, Lord my God, and will obey all Your requirements, laws, regulations, and commands. I will be careful to obey all the commands You give me; I will show love to You by walking in Your ways and clinging to You. Now, Lord Jesus Christ, prepare me for works of service, so that Your body may be built up. (Prov. 8:17; Ex. 20:6; Deut. 11:1, 22 NLT; Eph. 4:12 paraphrased)

Prayers, Praises, and Personal Notes

_____

_____

_____

_____

Scripture Reading: John 21:11-19

Practicing the Spiritual Life

What did Jesus ask Peter, and what did He command Peter to do in order to surrender His life to the Lord and serve Him?

_____

_____

_____

Whom do you need to love and take care of for Jesus' sake?

_____

_____

_____

Prayer

O Lord my God, I choose to love You and to obey You and commit myself to You, for You are my life. I will serve You wholeheartedly, serving You, Lord, not people. I will care for Your flock entrusted to me. I will watch over it willingly, not grudgingly—not for what I will get out of it, but because I am eager to serve You. I won't lord it over people assigned to my care, but will lead them by my good example. And then, Great Shepherd, when You come, my reward will be a never-ending share in Your glory and honor. (Deut. 30:20a NLT; Eph. 6:7; 1 Peter 5:2-4 NLT paraphrased)

Prayers, Praises, and Personal Notes

_____

_____

_____

_____

_____

Scripture Reading: Acts 9:1-22

Practicing the Spiritual Life

What did God use to help Saul surrender to His call? How quickly did Saul yield himself to the Lord, and what did he do?

_____

_____

_____

Is there any area of your life that you need to submit to the Lord in order to do His will and serve Him?

_____

_____

_____

Prayer

Lord God Almighty, I will seek good, not evil, that I may live. Then You will be with me. For I know I am loved by You, Lord, that You have chosen me, because the Gospel has come to me not simply with words, but also with power, with the Holy Spirit and with deep conviction. Therefore, I will imitate You, Lord, and those who genuinely love and serve You; in spite of severe suffering, I will welcome the message of the Gospel with the joy given me by the Holy Spirit. As a result, may I become an example to all Christians. And now may Your Word, Lord, ring out from me to people everywhere. (Amos 5:14a; 1 Thess. 1:4-5a, 6; 1 Thess. 1:7a, 8a NLT paraphrased)

Prayers, Praises, and Personal Notes

_____

_____

_____

Scripture Reading: 2 Timothy 2:1-10

Practicing the Spiritual Life

With regard to serving the Lord, of what did Paul remind Timothy? How did Paul exhort him?

_____

_____

_____

How did this passage speak to you about serving the Lord?

_____

_____

_____

Prayer

Lord Jesus, put Your words in my mouth and cover me with the shadow of Your hand—You who set the heavens in place, who laid the foundations of the earth. You are on my side; I will not fear: what can people do to me? If I suffer as a Christian, I will not be ashamed, but praise You, Lord, that I bear Your name. "For I am not ashamed of this Good News about Christ. It is the power of God at work, saving everyone who believes—Jews first and also Gentiles." "I know very well how foolish the message of the cross sounds to those who are on the road to destruction. But we who are being saved recognize this message as the very power of God." (Isa. 51:16a; Ps. 118:6 KJV; 1 Peter 4:16 paraphrased; Rom. 1:16 NLT; 1 Cor. 1:18 NLT not paraphrased)

Prayers, Praises, and Personal Notes

_____

_____

_____

Scripture Reading: Jeremiah 1

Practicing the Spiritual Life

When did the Lord set Jeremiah apart to do His will? Did Jeremiah think he was qualified to do what God wanted?

_____

_____

_____

How did this passage speak to you about releasing your life to God for His service no matter what He might ask of you?

_____

_____

_____

Prayer

Lord, this is what You told me: "Obey Me, and I will be Your God, and You will be mine. Only do as I say, and all will be well!" I will carefully obey all the commands You give me. I will not add to them or subtract from them. I will listen to You. For You created me and have cared for me since before I was born. You will be my God throughout my lifetime—until my hair is white with age. You made me, and You will care for me. You will carry me along and rescue me. I will not be afraid, for You are with me. (Jer. 7:23 NLT; Deut. 12:32 NLT; Isa. 46:3-4 NLT; 43:5a NLT paraphrased)

Prayers, Praises, and Personal Notes

_____

_____

_____

_____

_____

_____

_____

_____

_____

_____

_____

_____

_____

_____

_____

_____

_____

_____

_____

_____

_____

_____

_____

_____

_____

_____

_____

_____

_____

_____

WEEK EIGHT

Realize the Need to Change

*"I beseech you therefore, brethren, by the mercies of God,
that ye present your bodies a living sacrifice,
holy, acceptable unto God, which is your reasonable service.
And be not conformed to this world: but be ye transformed
by the renewing of your mind, that ye may prove
what is that good, and acceptable, and perfect will of God."*

ROMANS 12:1-2 KJV

*C*orrie ten Boom fell on the pavement near a phone booth and was unable to get up. After undergoing tests at the hospital, she was grateful she hadn't broken her hip. It was only bruised, but she would have to stay in bed for several weeks.

She was transferred to a clinic to recuperate. She soon became impatient and irritable because she was unable to move or turn without the assistance of a nurse. When she realized her hip was not going to heal in time for her to speak at a student conference in Germany, she asked friends to find someone to come and pray for her healing.

A minister came to her room that afternoon. She relates what happened. "Standing beside my bed, he said, 'Is there any unconfessed sin in your life?'

"What an odd question, I thought. I understood he had agreed to come pray for my healing, but was it his job to get so personal about my sins and attitudes? However, I did not have far to look. My impatience and demanding attitude toward my nurse had been wrong—very wrong. I asked her to come to the room, and I repented of my sin, asking both her and God to forgive me."[1]

Corrie realized that she needed to change as much as she needed to be healed. She went to Germany ten days later, and when she arrived, she recognized that God had used that time to prepare her for a difficult ministry. She needed to share the Gospel by the Holy Spirit's power, not her own.

Throughout her life Corrie continued to realize her need to change. She said, "I wish I could say that after a long and fruitful life traveling the world, I had learned to forgive all my enemies. I wish I could say that merciful and charitable thoughts just naturally flowed from me and on to others. But they don't. If there is one thing I've learned since I've passed my eightieth birthday, it's that I can't store up good feelings and behavior—but only draw them fresh from God every day."[2]

Realize Your Need for Real Change

To grow spiritually and make the changes necessary to become holy, we need to realize that transformation is a lifelong process. We need to daily draw afresh from the Holy Spirit's strength to change our character, conduct, and thought life.

We're more prepared to make real changes in our lives if we're willing to have a realistic view of ourselves. "Modern man, conscious of his tremendous scientific achievements in recent years, naturally inclines to a high opinion of himself. He views material wealth as in any case more important than moral character, and in the moral realm he is resolutely kind to himself, treating small virtues as compensating for great vices and refusing to take seriously the idea that, morally speaking, there is anything much wrong with him."[3]

We may not commit "major" sins, but we minimize "minor" weaknesses, chronic character defects, and habitual failure. We may repeat the same mistakes and continue in the same pattern of mishandling our lives and relationships. We don't seem to learn from them or make the necessary changes. Yet those very shortcomings may have devastating and long-term consequences in our own lives and the lives of others.

We may also have a false view of our spiritual condition, being either too kind to ourselves or too self-condemning, or we may lead double lives. We act in ways that are seriously hurting loved ones and other people; but among Christians we falsely present ourselves as committed believers. We put on the outward pretense of faithfully serving the Lord.

"In His rebuke to the Pharisees, our Lord declared a principle that must guide all our efforts to change into the person God wants us to be. He made it clear that there is no place for pretense. We must come to grips with what's going on behind the whitewashed appearance of our life. . . . To look honestly at those parts of our experience we naturally deny is painful business, so painful that the analogy of death is not too strong. But to change according to Christ's instructions requires us to face all we prefer to deny. *Real change requires an inside look*."[4]

If we're in denial, we fear what we may see inside ourselves. We close our eyes to our spiritual pretense. Or we may see inside ourselves, however, and be discouraged because our spiritual growth is too slow.[5]

I often wonder why the kind of transforming change that I need to make is so difficult. It requires far more concentrated effort than I am able to sustain over a long period of time. I may be well aware of what I need to do and may even know the steps to follow. I may be able to maintain the discipline for a while, but until I have a transformation of heart and am convinced in the deepest part of myself, I seem to easily fall back.

Sometimes I come to a complete standstill spiritually. Other times I regress, and the sins that I thought I had overcome resurface. Sometimes I feel as if I haven't made any changes for a long period of time, and then I turn a corner and can see how God has been working in my life.

The times that I have experienced sudden and swift transformation have been rare but powerful and have radically changed the course of my life. For the most part, the significant changes and spiritual growth have come about through painful heartaches, unresolved trials, and serious breakdowns in important relationships.

I'm aware of changes in my life that yet need to be made, and I'm sure that I'm blind to others, but I know the Lord will reveal them in His time. Some changes that the Lord desires me to make seem so difficult and frustrating I wonder if I'll ever succeed.

"The greatest burden we have to carry in life is self; the most difficult thing we have to manage is self. Our own daily living, our frames and feelings, our special weaknesses and temptations, our peculiar temperaments, our inward affairs of every kind—these are the things that perplex and worry us more than anything else and that bring us most frequently into bondage and darkness."[6]

To be freed from this bondage, we must be freed from our preoccupation with ourselves. Genuine spiritual change will come about as we continuously surrender the burden of self to the Lord's care and keeping.

We must relinquish to Him our character defects and weaknesses; our particular type of personality; our view of ourselves; our feelings of inferiority, indifference, or superiority.[7] "The fact is, God helps the helpless, the undeserving, those who don't measure up, those who fail to achieve His standard."[8]

He made us and understands us, and we must trust Him to accomplish His purposes for our lives. We may be confident that the Lord will continue to change us into the people He desires us to be as long as we surrender our will to His, as long as we're transparent before Him about our sins, as long as we daily draw on His transforming power.

"Sincere, seeking persons should be 'drawn' by hope, joy, and desire and should not be 'driven' by the experience of slavish fear. Neither should they be overcome by anxiety, even because of the sin that remains in them. Their hope in Christ is always greater than their despair and should drive them all the more to the promises and the love of Christ, which will bring them the cleansing and freedom they desire."[9]

As we avail ourselves of our Lord's promises and His tender, loving forgiveness, we'll experience cleansing and healing. It's only then that genuine change comes about and the spiritual renewal that He so desires for us.

Reaffirm Your Need to Be Spiritually Renewed

Real change means we commit ourselves to the ongoing process of being renewed and transformed. How do we experience spiritual renewal? First, we begin by constantly changing old attitudes and developing new patterns of thinking. We seek to know the mind of Christ through His Word. When the Holy Spirit convicts us of wrong thinking, we renounce our sinful mind-set and humbly seek to have a Christlike attitude.

Second, we'll experience spiritual renewal as we seek to lead a sanctified life. This means we separate ourselves from sinful practices and the profanities of this world and set ourselves apart to serve the Lord according to His will and purposes for us.

"Sanctification means that we are being renewed in accordance with the image of God—that, in other words, we are becoming more like God, or like Christ, who is the perfect image of God. Our renewal in the image of God, however, may be viewed from two angles: as the work of God in us and as a process in which we are actively engaged."[10]

Third, we grow spiritually and are cleansed by God's Word as we study, meditate upon it, follow its precepts, and rely upon its equipping power to strengthen us to serve the Lord. Scripture is one of the most essential means whereby we are trained to be godly.[11] "All Scripture is God-breathed and is useful for teaching, rebuking, correcting and training in righteousness, so that the man of God may be thoroughly equipped for every good work" (2 Tim. 3:16-17). Moreover, we are cleansed and transformed by God's Word, as promised in Ephesians 5:25-27: "Christ loved the church and gave himself up for her to make her holy, cleansing her by the washing with water through the word, and to present her to himself as a radiant church, without stain or wrinkle or any other blemish, but holy and blameless."

Fourth, as we demonstrate the fruit of the Spirit in our lives, we're spiritually renewed and reflect the life of Christ in such a way that we show forth His attributes. "The fruit of the Spirit is love, joy, peace, patience, kindness, goodness, faithfulness, gentleness and self-control. Against such things there is no law" (Gal. 5:22-23). God expects more than belief in Christian virtues but an actual living reality. "By their fruits ye shall know them" (Matt. 7:20 KJV).

Recognize Your Need for Integrity

Godliness requires that we develop and maintain integrity, one of the most vital attributes of a sincerely spiritual person. After Job's ten children had been killed and he had lost his immense wealth, Satan came before God. "Then the Lord said to Satan, 'Have you considered my servant Job? There is no one on earth like him; he is blameless and upright, a man who fears God and shuns evil. And he still maintains his integrity, though you incited me against him to ruin him without any reason'" (Job 2:3).

When Job lost everything, he kept his spiritual integrity. In holy humility, he tore his robe, shaved his head, and laid facedown on the ground in grief and submission before God.

He worshiped the Lord, saying that he had nothing when he was born, and he would have nothing when He died, and if God wanted to take everything away, He had the right to do so. Then Job praised the Lord and did not charge Him with wrongdoing (Job 1:20-22).

We may be confused about what it means to be holy. We may believe that godly people do not openly grieve or question why they are experiencing terrible trials, that they demonstrate godliness by not expressing sorrow but by spiritualizing their heartaches and praising God for their difficulties. That is not true at all.

Job was very much an earthly person who grieved deeply, questioned why he had suffered such tragedies, examined his own heart and life for sin, and desperately begged for answers from God. The distinction is that Job did not turn away from his faith or accuse God of wrongdoing. Job was pure of heart before God and yet purely human in his grief.

Here is a secret of a transformed life: We're called to be people of integrity by revering the Lord during good times and bad.

Humble integrity means we recognize our position before God.

Everything we have came from Him. The Lord has a right to give or take away and to allow trials to come into our lives.

Crying out in pain and seeking for answers from God are not the same as accusing Him of wrongdoing and blaming Him for our hurts, losses, and "senseless" tragedies. At the same time, we do not minimize the severity of our trials by blessing the Lord's name, offering sacrificial praise, and worshiping Him. We may express gratitude to the Lord for His comforting presence while being in deep pain.

Grief and praise are not contradictory but complimentary. When we openly work through the grieving process, we're healed and spiritually changed; when we magnify the Lord in our sorrow, we're uplifted by our praise and thanksgiving. We're relieved of despair and released to hope.

Holy integrity also means we're committed to spiritual purity, ethical business practices, and moral and personal integrity. This means we're to be blameless, upright, and pure of heart, abstaining from evil (Job 2:3). We act with simplicity, honesty, and sincerity in our dealings with others. We do not use pretense, guile, deceitful cunning, or duplicity, which make us double-minded in action and speech.

Integrity means that we do not live by a double standard. For example, we may expect prompt payment from those who owe us a debt, but we defraud others by not paying what we owe them, by being chronically delinquent, or by being financially irresponsible. We must be honest and sincere. We must not pretend to do what is right while being corrupt in our practices. Genuine integrity is genuine holiness.

Resolve to Change Without Changing Others

Real spiritual change can only come about in our lives as we're willing to be transformed and grow in godliness without seeing a change in other people. We seek personal and spiritual transformation because of what God will do in our lives, not for what He will do in someone else. If we change because we expect God to transform others, we'll be disappointed every time. Our desire for people to change may be for their highest and best interest, but they may remain the same.

My father and stepmother were violent alcoholics, but though I prayed for them for many years, they both died in that condition. I felt grief and a tremendous sense of loss that our relationship had been so difficult, painful, and stressful. Above all, I missed not having a Christian relationship with them.

God in His tender grace gradually healed me of the hurts I experienced as a child and as an adult. He gave me the ability to go on with my life without being stuck in my grief over their destroyed lives. When others don't change, God gives us the grace to accept what to us is the unacceptable.

To experience genuine spiritual change in our own lives, we need to relinquish our expectations about how others will be changed. That doesn't mean we stop praying; we must continue to intercede on their behalf while at the same time releasing them to the Lord's care.

We must realize that we're not their Savior; Christ alone is their Redeemer. Too often we think we can change people, and instead we enable them to continue in their self-destruction. All our energy may be consumed in trying to save others rather than yielding ourselves to the Lord so that He may change us.

We may also feel that if others see how God is changing us and working in our lives, they will surely come to know Him or commit themselves to Him. God may do a marvelous work of transformation in us, but that does not mean others will desire to know Christ. Jesus' ministry was one of caring, healing, and demonstrating love. He gave His very life to save us, and yet He was and still is rejected and despised.

May we not lose heart. Let us maintain our hope in the faithfulness of our Lord. He is transforming our own and others' lives by His grace and mercy.

Finally, we'll become more Christlike as we reflect more of Him and less of ourselves. One of the most powerful promises of His renewing work in our lives is found in 2 Corinthians 3:18: "And we, who with unveiled faces all reflect the Lord's glory, are being transformed into his likeness with ever-increasing glory, which comes from the Lord, who is the Spirit."

"People should be seeing something of the glory of Christ when they look at us. As we're reflecting that glory, however, we're also being transformed into that same image—that is, into the likeness of Christ—from one degree of glory to another. As we continually reflect the glory of Christ, we're continually being transformed into His image."[12]

Scripture Reading: Nehemiah 1:1-11

Practicing the Spiritual Life

How did Nehemiah respond when he heard about the spiritual condition of the Jewish exiles? What did Nehemiah confess, and what did he ask the Lord to do?

_____

_____

_____

We need to have a realistic view of our spiritual condition in order to be transformed. In what way did this passage speak to you about confessing your sins and making changes in your own life?

_____

_____

_____

Prayer

Forgiving Savior, streams of tears flow from my eyes, for I have not obeyed Your Word. Before I was afflicted I went astray, but now I will obey Your Word. I acknowledge my sin to You; I will not cover up my iniquity. I confess my transgressions to You, so that You will forgive the guilt of my sin. For I have been chosen according to Your foreknowledge, Father, through the sanctifying work of Your Spirit, for obedience to You, Jesus Christ, and sprinkling by Your blood. For it is in You that I have redemption through Your blood and the forgiveness of my sins, in accordance with the riches of Your grace, O God. (Ps. 119:136, 67; 32:5; 1 Peter 1:2a; Eph. 1:7 paraphrased)

Prayers, Praises, and Personal Notes

_____

_____

_____

Scripture Reading: Matthew 22:15-21

Practicing the Spiritual Life

How were the Pharisees falsely religious? What compliments did they give Jesus about Himself? Do you think the Pharisees really meant what they said?

_____

_____

_____

Are you aware of any spiritual pretenses or falseness in your own life? If so, in what ways do you need to change?

_____

_____

_____

Prayer

O God of Truth, deliver me from having a tongue that is a deadly arrow and speaks deceit. May I not speak cordially to my neighbors but in my heart set a trap for them. Deliver me from being false and unfaithful, and from not returning to You with all my heart but only in pretense. Rather help me to be among the righteous who hate what is false, and not among the wicked who bring shame and disgrace. Then true instruction will be in my mouth, and nothing false will be found on my lips, so that I may walk with You in peace and uprightness and turn many from sin. (Jer. 9:8; 3:10; Prov. 13:5; Mal. 2:6 paraphrased)

Prayers, Praises, and Personal Notes

_____

_____

_____

_____

Scripture Reading: Romans 12:1-2

Practicing the Spiritual Life

What specific steps are we to take to be transformed? What will we be able to know and prove as a result?

_____

_____

_____

To make real changes, what steps do you need to take in order to submit yourself to the ongoing process of being transformed?

_____

_____

_____

Prayer

Merciful Lord, I will not lose heart. Though outwardly I am wasting away, yet inwardly I am being renewed day by day. For I know that my body is Your temple, Holy Spirit, and that You are in me, and that I received You from God. I am not my own; I was bought at a price. Therefore, I will honor You with my body. And by the power that enables You to bring everything under Your control, transform my lowly body so that it will be like Your glorious body. (2 Cor. 4:16; 1 Cor. 6:19-20; Phil. 3:21 paraphrased)

Prayers, Praises, and Personal Notes

_____

_____

_____

_____

_____

Scripture Reading: Psalm 119:9-11; 2 Timothy 3:16-17

Practicing the Spiritual Life

We are sanctified by God's Word. How do these passages say we are spiritually renewed and equipped to lead a changed life?

_____

_____

_____

Make a specific commitment for a certain period of time to study Scripture, asking the Lord to use specific passages to speak to your heart, transform your life, and equip you for service.

_____

_____

_____

Prayer

"Your word, O Lord, is eternal; it stands firm in the heavens." And I have been born again, not of perishable seed, but of imperishable, through the living and enduring Word of God. Your Word is quick and powerful, sharper than any two-edged sword, piercing even to the dividing asunder of my soul and spirit, and of my joints and marrow, and is a discerner of my thoughts and intents of my heart. Therefore, I will apply my heart to instruction and my ears to words of knowledge. "Give me understanding, and I will keep your law and obey it with all my heart." (Ps. 119:89 not paraphrased; 1 Peter 1:23; Heb. 4:12 KJV; Prov. 23:12 paraphrased; Ps. 119:34 not paraphrased)

Prayers, Praises, and Personal Notes

_____

_____

_____

Scripture Reading: Colossians 1:3-12

Practicing the Spiritual Life

We are spiritually renewed as we demonstrate the fruit of the Spirit in our lives. According to Paul's prayers, what are some of the specific ways we are to lead a changed and fruitful life?

_____

_____

_____

What specifically spoke to you from this passage about leading a changed life and demonstrating the fruit of the Spirit?

_____

_____

_____

Prayer

Jesus, You are the vine; I am the branch. If I remain in You and You in me, I will bear much fruit; apart from You I can do nothing. I did not choose You, but You chose me and appointed me to go and bear fruit—fruit that will last. Then, Father, You will give me whatever I ask in Jesus' name. Lord, this is to Your Father's glory, that I bear much fruit, showing myself to be Your disciple. Therefore, I will be filled with the fruit of righteousness that comes through You, Jesus Christ—to Your glory and praise, O God. (John 15:5, 16, 8; Phil. 1:11 paraphrased)

Prayers, Praises, and Personal Notes

_____

_____

_____

_____

Scripture Reading: 1 Kings 9:1-7

Practicing the Spiritual Life

What did God exhort Solomon to do in order to lead a holy life? God warned Solomon that he and his sons should not make certain changes. What were they?

_____

_____

_____

One of the most essential attributes of a godly person is integrity. In what areas of your life would you like to have more integrity?

_____

_____

_____

Prayer

I know, my God, that You test my heart and are pleased with integrity. Therefore, I will give all things to You willingly and with honest intent. May I be upright so that I may be guided by integrity; may I not be found unfaithful; otherwise, I will be destroyed by my duplicity. For if I am a person of integrity, I will walk securely; but if I take crooked paths, I will be found out. "May integrity and uprightness protect me, because my hope is in you." (1 Chron. 29:17a; Prov. 11:3; 10:9 paraphrased; Ps. 25:21 not paraphrased)

Prayers, Praises, and Personal Notes

_____

_____

_____

_____

_____

Scripture Reading: Luke 6:41-45

Practicing the Spiritual Life

What do verses 41 and 42 say about changing ourselves before we try to change others? How do the remaining verses contrast the differences in fruit-bearing?

_____

_____

_____

Is there someone that you desire to change? Release that person to the Lord. What changes would the Lord have *you* make?

_____

_____

_____

Prayer

May I have the wisdom, Lord, that comes from heaven, which is first of all pure, then peace-loving, considerate, submissive, full of mercy and good fruit, impartial and sincere. May I be a peacemaker, who by sowing in peace raises a harvest of righteousness. Help me to encourage others, so that we may build each other up. And I will respect those who work hard for You, Lord, who are over me in the Lord and who admonish me. I will hold them in the highest regard in love because of their work. I will live in peace with others. I will make sure that I do not pay back wrong for wrong, but I will always try to be kind to Christians and to everyone else. (James 3:17-18; 1 Thess. 5:11a, 12-13 paraphrased)

Prayers, Praises, and Personal Notes

_____

_____

_____

_____

_____

_____

_____

_____

_____

_____

_____

_____

_____

_____

_____

_____

_____

_____

_____

_____

_____

_____

_____

_____

_____

WEEK NINE

Rely on God's Guidance

"Good and upright is the Lord;
therefore he instructs sinners in his ways.
He guides the humble in what is right
and teaches them his way.
All the ways of the Lord are
loving and faithful for those who
keep the demands of his covenant."

PSALM 25:8-10

*M*y husband can drive almost anywhere without a map. He has this built-in radar. If he's been to a place one time, he remembers how to get there again. Not me. I may need written directions after I've been to a place two or three times. If I get turned around, I can get lost in a familiar place.

Rely on God's Guidance for Moral Decisions

Just as we need clear directions, signs, and a map to travel to unfamiliar places, we need to know how to follow God's map, recognize identifying landmarks, and rely on His guidance on the journey to holiness.

This journey requires us to make many decisions, and we need the Lord's guidance to make godly choices. The kinds of decisions we make fall into two basic categories: moral and nonmoral personal decisions.[1] The Bible is our source of direction regarding God's moral will. It outlines for us a clear route to follow.

In the following passages, note that there are no distinctions between "minor" or "major" sins, such as jealousy or drunkenness; and sexual sin is only one of many different kinds of immoral choices.

"But among you there must not be even a hint of sexual immorality, or of any kind of impurity, or of greed, because these are improper for God's holy people. Nor should there be obscenity, foolish talk or coarse joking, which are out of place, but rather thanksgiving. For of this you can be sure: No immoral, impure or greedy person—such a man is an idolater—has any inheritance in the kingdom of Christ and of God" (Eph. 5:3-5). "Let us behave decently, as in the daytime, not in orgies and drunkenness, not in sexual immorality and debauchery, not in dissension and jealousy" (Rom. 13:13).

The demands of God's moral will are very clear. Yet we may fail to view God's laws as unchanging absolutes. We may devise numerous rationalizations for making immoral choices.

Rather than basing our decisions on God's Word, we may make them based on our own belief systems, driving passions, what is culturally acceptable, and on what other people are doing. We may also make moral decisions depending on our moods, whims, pressure of circumstances or people, or on what is expedient.

We are daily challenged to follow God's moral will. Yet we may not think about whether our choices are moral because they've become a normal part of our behavior and thinking processes. Though we may deny, minimize, or rationalize immoral choices, we're still responsible to the Lord regarding the decisions we make. We may be the most self-deceived and vulnerable to Satan's attacks when it comes to making this kind of decision. But we need to remember that God's moral absolutes are meant to keep us from self-destruction rather than deprive us of pleasure.

Recently, I deceived myself about a "minor moral" choice that I made. My college staff parking sticker had expired. I rationalized that I was only teaching two hours on campus. Every week I felt convicted as I illegally parked my car in designated staff parking. I could have bought a fifty-cent parking permit from a nearby machine for the two hours, but I didn't do that either.

The fifth week I was feeling very convicted and was thinking that I should buy the fifty-cent permit, or I was going to get a citation. But I again ignored the Holy Spirit's warning. When I came out from class, I had a ticket on my windshield with a strong reprimand about deliberately parking illegally.

My greatest shock was how calculating my decision had been. Here I was writing this chapter on making moral decisions, and I had deliberately made the immoral choice not to buy a permit. The next day I paid my eighteen-dollar fine and my twenty dollars for a staff parking permit. This experience made me realize how easy it is to rationalize sinful choices.

Rely on God's Guidance for Personal Decisions

The second kind of decision for which we may seek God's guidance are nonmoral and personal. "Complex decisions include major questions such as what profession to choose, what college to attend, whether or not to marry and where to go to church. They also include decisions about priorities: how should you spend your time and money?"[2]

If we're going to grow in godliness, we need to realize that we face critical personal decisions throughout our lifetime. Yet how often do we make life-changing decisions without relying on God's direction? We may not think about asking Him for guidance, or if we do, we may be afraid we won't like what He'll ask of us.

When we're trying to make critical personal decisions, we may feel a great weight of responsibility. The heaviest weight that will sink us every time, however, is our determination that God endorse the decisions we've already set our hearts on. We may not desire His guidance as much as we desire His approval.

We may also feel we must be in control of our lives. We want to determine what's going to happen to us.

On the other hand, if we sincerely seek God's guidance about a decision, we may become anxious that we won't understand His will and make the wrong choice. But God is more than willing to guide us as long as we genuinely desire to know His will.

The Conditions for Receiving Guidance

To become godly, we need to realize that every promise of guidance includes a condition and a responsibility to meet. Elisabeth Elliot said, "Often I have prayed to God for light, and he has shown me some promise in the Bible which indicates that he will certainly give me the light I am asking for, if—and then I have found, to my despair, that a great deal is asked of me in exchange."[3]

The conditions God requires are for our benefit and spiritual maturity. They are not meant to hinder us in the decision-making process.

The first condition is faith—believing that God will guide us. "Trust in the Lord with all your heart; do not depend on your own understanding. Seek his will in all you do, and he will direct your paths" (Prov. 3:5-6 NLT). We see in this passage three steps to follow. We need to set aside our fears and place our complete confidence in the Lord. Next we must let go of our need to understand and be in control. Finally, we need to seek the Lord's will, not just about the decision we desire to make, but during the entire process. We're to acknowledge Him in all our ways. We're to seek His will not only for the major decisions but in everything we do.

The second condition for guidance is that we recognize our sinful condition. "Good and upright is the Lord; therefore he instructs sinners in his ways. He guides the humble in what is right and teaches them his way. All the ways of the Lord are loving and faithful for those who keep the demands of his covenant" (Ps. 25:8-10). We don't have to be sinless to have God's guidance; we have to be willing to be freed from sin. We must also realize the Lord is good and righteous and will never lead us to do any sort of wrong.

The third condition for guidance is that we humble ourselves before the Lord. The decisions we need to make may hinge on a matter of pride. For example, we may need a job, and we've set our minds on a certain kind of work at a particular salary. We've found a good job at a lower wage that seems perfectly suited to us, and we know it's the job the Lord has provided. But instead of being humble and grateful for God's provision, we may be disappointed because we wanted something far better. We need to humble ourselves and graciously receive what God allows or desires for us.

The fourth condition is that we keep the demands of His covenant, which is to obey His Word and do as the Lord desires. We cannot dictate our terms to the Lord. Rather we covenant with Him to meet *His* requirements. "Our Lord never dictated to His Father, and we are not here to dictate to God; we are here to submit to His will so that He may work through us what He wants. When we realize this, He will make us broken bread and poured-out wine to feed and nourish others."[4]

The fifth condition is self-denial. If we will come after Christ, let us deny ourselves, and take up our cross, and follow Him (Matt.16:24b KJV). Following Him and depending on His guidance begins with "I will."

We need to carry the cross that Jesus asks us to take up on His behalf. This cross is our own, and no one else may carry it for us, and we may not carry anyone else's cross. We're to lay down our preconceived ideas of how God should or will guide us both now and in the future. To take up our cross and follow Him means to take up our own difficulties, trials, and sufferings.[5]

As we do so, we'll learn what it means to sacrifice our own choices for the Lord's, deny our own will, and submit ourselves to His guiding hand. But we don't have to carry our cross alone: Jesus bears it with us.[6]

We can depend upon Him for strength to bear our trials and do what He desires of us. "He becomes to us what we cannot be in ourselves. We find ourselves possessed with a power that is not ours, and a holiness that is not ours either—but all His, who lives in us."[7]

In denying ourselves, we need to realize also that God's guidance is not meant for our benefit alone but for others as well. When the Lord directs us,

He has far more in mind than our personal needs. Everything that happens to us is not for or about us.

We may ask the Lord for guidance and find ourselves in a place we would never have chosen. We may wonder if we missed God's direction because where He put us and the trials we're experiencing make no sense to us. We may wonder, "Why am I here? What does this have to do with me?"

The Lord may be saying, "What you are experiencing on the route I am taking you has little to do with you. It has everything to do with how you need to serve others."

This is what it means to deny ourselves for the sake of Christ. We need to stop looking inward and being concerned about ourselves and start looking outward and watching for what the Lord desires us to do for His sake.

The sixth condition for guidance is to obey God's Word and follow scriptural principles to make our decisions. At this point, we may want to cry out, as Elisabeth Elliot did: "I cannot fulfill the conditions. I do not 'keep instruction.' I hardly listen to it, in fact. I am not 'godly.' I am not good or meek or upright or blameless or truthful or self-sacrificing. . . . Even a casual look at God's word shows me that a relative goodness won't do. I am none of the things I am told I need to be in order to expect God's guidance."[8]

Jesus Is the Way

Though meeting God's conditions may seem impossible to us, He has provided the means to do so. "The truth is that the whole thing has been done for us—Jesus is our guide, and he is himself the way."[9]

"He is both the Way itself and the One who walks beside us on that Way, bearing on His shoulders the responsibility for our affairs. We can go shopping with Jesus, go to work with Him, do the most menial tasks in the house with Him, and undertake the largest responsibilities in our profession with Him. If we are cleansed from our sin as we go, we shall many times a day turn to Him to seek His guidance, to ask His help, or just to praise Him for His love and sufficiency."[10]

Even when we may not be aware of His guiding presence, even when we disobey Him, Jesus is still the Way. We may not follow Him, we may aimlessly wander spiritually, we may turn and go in the wrong direction, but that does not change the fact that He is the Way. He will accomplish His will whether we obey or not. Our disobedience cannot hinder His plans and purposes, as the following passage states: "I make known the end from the beginning, from ancient times, what is still to come. I say: My purpose will stand, and I will do all that I please. From the east I summon a bird of prey; from a far-off land, a man to fulfill my purpose. What I have said, that will I bring about; what I have planned, that will I do" (Isa. 46:10-11).

By our obedience we become a part of God's unfolding purposes. "Therefore, my dear friends, as you have always obeyed—not only in my presence, but now much more in my absence—continue to work out your salvation with fear and trembling, for it is God who works in you to will and to act according to his good purpose" (Phil. 2:12-13).

The Means by Which God Guides Us

Scripture is the guidebook for both moral and nonmoral personal decisions. Most of our questions about guidance are answered there. The secret to becoming a godly person and knowing God's will is to consistently read His Word. "The unfolding of your words gives light; it gives understanding to the simple" (Ps. 119:130).

By simple, childlike faith we may rely on the light of Scripture to guide us. But how often do we complicate scriptural commands with spiritual rationalizations or complex intellectual or psychological arguments? The more we study the Word and simply apply it to our lives, the easier it will become to follow God's guidance.

Biblical commands regarding moral decisions are clear. When making nonmoral personal decisions, we may rely on the principles and truths of Scripture to give us direction. Often Scripture may guide us even though we don't receive a direct answer regarding the choice we should make.

In any event, we must be careful about making decisions based on strong feelings or a sense of urgency without gaining sound confirmation. "Earnest Christians seeking guidance often go wrong about it. Why is this? Often the reason is that their notion of the nature and method of divine guidance is distorted. They look for a will-o'-the-wisp; they overlook the guidance that is ready at hand, and lay themselves open to all sorts of delusions. Their basic mistake is to think of guidance as essentially *inward prompting by the Holy Spirit apart from the written Word.*[11]

We may be guided by inward prompting, but we must be cautious that we don't deceive ourselves because we want something so much. We must not use Scripture to justify ungodly choices. We may say, "I have peace about this decision."

Personal peace by itself is not a reliable indicator that we are following God's directions at all. We need to be careful that we do not twist the meaning of the Word to fortify us in making wrong choices. We may make tragic decisions and say we're in the will of God. We may convince ourselves and others that God was guiding us when everything we were doing was contrary to Scripture and God's moral will.

If we truly desire to receive God's guidance, a strong sense of doubt about the rightness of our decision is a critical warning signal that we need to heed. When we're following His directions, we'll have a God-given peace and ample confirmation.

The Lord guides us by many other means as we depend on Him.[12] We need to be prepared for God to ask us to be faithful to the duties and ministry we've already been called to do, rather than hoping He will lead us to do something else. He may lead us by timing—*His* time, not ours.

He may use others to give us the perspective and wisdom we need. "Where no counsel is, the people fall: but in the multitude of counselors there is safety" (Prov. 11:14 KJV). We also need to consider our abilities, gifts, and the direction our life seems to be taking us.[13]

Common sense and circumstances are another means of guidance.[14] Ron's and my decision to move from Orange County was motivated by our circumstances—an unsafe neighborhood. Common sense and the doctor also told us that Ron needed to get out of his high-stress job. He has done far better now that he is working under less pressure and does not have to travel long distances on congested freeways.

The Lord may also impress certain desires upon our hearts. This may be the most confusing means, since it is difficult to distinguish between our own determination and the Holy Spirit's urgings. Ron and I both wanted to move to Santa Maria. The desire grew stronger and stronger over time, but we weren't sure whether it was our own desperation or God's will leading us.

Prior to our move, three friends who have no relationship with each other separately told us that they felt strongly that God was going to move us to Santa Maria. But it wasn't until we were living here for more than a year that I was certain it was God's will. The Lord has confirmed in numerous different ways that we came here by His guiding hand.

I'm a cautious doubter by nature, so trusting the Lord to guide me has never been easy. In most respects caution has saved me immense heartache, while doubt has crippled me and unnecessarily prolonged decisions or caused me to question the ones I made.

I have come to realize that heartaches and difficulties are not an indicator that I am out of the Lord's will. In fact, many times trials have become more intense as I was doing exactly what God wanted. At the same time, I try to examine my own life to make sure that I have not caused my own trials and/or sinned in some way.

After we have earnestly prayed, read the Word, sought direction and godly counsel, this is the ultimate bottom line: We make personal decisions by faith. Once we make a decision, we may, however, need to change or modify it as we gain spiritual insight and greater understanding of a situation or relationship. Changing a decision is not a sign of failure; it may well be a sign of spiritual wisdom and the means by which the Holy Spirit is guiding us.

Though we do not know the route we'll be taking on our spiritual journey, we may rely on the Lord to show us the way. For He has promised: "Whether you turn to the right or to the left, your ears will hear a voice behind you, saying, 'This is the way; walk in it'" (Isa. 30:21).

Scripture Reading: Psalm 25:4-7

Practicing the Spiritual Life

What do we need to ask the Lord to show us when we're seeking guidance?

_____

_____

_____

What is the most critical moral or nonmoral personal decision that you need to make at this time? Write what you need the Lord to show you so you can make your decision, and what you desire Him to remember as you rely on His guidance.

_____

_____

_____

Prayer

"Teach me your way, O Lord, and I will walk in your truth; give me an undivided heart that I may fear your name." "Show mercy to me according to your great love." "If you are pleased with me, teach me your ways so I may know you and continue to find favor with you." "Guide me with your counsel." "Send forth your light and your truth, let them guide me; let them bring me to your holy mountain, to the place where you dwell." (Ps. 86:11; Neh. 13:22; Ex. 33:13a; Ps. 73:24a; 43:3 not paraphrased)

Prayers, Praises, and Personal Notes

_____

_____

_____

_____

Scripture Reading: Psalm 25:8-12

Practicing the Spiritual Life

Whom does the Lord instruct in the ways He has chosen for them?

_____

_____

_____

What does your attitude and condition need to be so that the Lord may guide you in the way He has chosen?

_____

_____

_____

Prayer

Lord, You are upright; You are my Rock. Help me, O God my Savior, for the glory of Your name; deliver me and forgive my sins for Your name's sake. For You sustain the humble but cast the wicked to the ground. "Teach me, and I will be quiet; show me where I have been wrong." "Teach me to do your will, for you are my God; may your good Spirit lead me on level ground." I will praise, You, Lord, who counsels me; even at night my heart will instruct me. (Ps. 92:15a; 79:9; 147:6 paraphrased; Job 6:24; Ps. 143:10 not paraphrased; Ps.16:7 paraphrased)

Prayers, Praises, and Personal Notes

_____

_____

_____

_____

_____

Scripture Reading: Proverbs 3:5-6; 20:24

Practicing the Spiritual Life

What do we need to do to receive direction? What does this passage say we don't understand?

_____

_____

_____

In what ways do you need the Lord to direct your steps as you work through the decision-making process?

_____

_____

_____

Prayer

Who endowed my heart with wisdom or gave understanding to my mind? Your inspiration, Almighty, gives me understanding. "Your hands made me and formed me; give me understanding to learn your commands." My heart is in Your hand, Lord, as are the water courses; direct and turn my heart whichever way You will. I know, O Lord, that my life is not my own; it is not for me to direct my steps. "Let the morning bring me word of your unfailing love, for I have put my trust in you. Show me the way I should go, for to you I lift up my soul." (Job 38:36; Job 32:8b KJV paraphrased; Ps. 119:73 not paraphrased; Prov. 21:1 AMP; Jer. 10:23 paraphrased; Ps. 143:8 not paraphrased)

Prayers, Praises, and Personal Notes

_____

_____

_____

_____

Scripture Reading: Psalm 119:130; Isaiah 30:21

Practicing the Spiritual Life

What are some of the ways the Lord guides us?

_____

_____

_____

Ask the Lord to guide and speak to you through the Word of God as you read it and seek His direction. Write out those passages that the Lord is using to guide you.

_____

_____

_____

Prayer

"I trust in you, O Lord; I say, 'You are my God.'" "Let me understand the teaching of your precepts; then I will meditate on your wonders." "Open my eyes that I may see wonderful things in your law." "Direct my footsteps according to your word; let no sin rule over me." O my Redeemer, the Holy One of Israel: You are the Lord my God, who teaches me what is best for me, who directs me in the way I should go. (Ps. 31:14; 119:27, 18, 133 not paraphrased; Isa. 48:17 paraphrased)

Prayers, Praises, and Personal Notes

_____

_____

_____

_____

_____

Scripture Reading: Acts 21:4-14

Practicing the Spiritual Life

What counsel did Paul receive about going to Jerusalem? What did he decide by faith? What did the Christians say in releasing Paul to follow God's guidance?

_____

_____

_____

If you have a difficult decision to make, write down what you believe the Lord would have you do. From whom can you seek sound spiritual counsel to help you make your decision?

_____

_____

_____

Prayer

To You, O God, belong wisdom and power; counsel and understanding are Yours. Therefore, I will make plans by seeking advice; I will obtain guidance. Otherwise my plans will fail if I lack counsel, but with many advisers they will succeed. Your testimonies also are my delight and my counselors. Lord, teach me sound judgment and knowledge, for I believe in Your commandments. Instruct me and teach me in the way I should go; counsel me and watch over me. (Job 12:13; Prov. 20:18; 15:22; Ps. 119:24, 66 KJV; Ps. 32:8 paraphrased)

Prayers, Praises, and Personal Notes

_____

_____

_____

Scripture Reading: James 1:19-25

Practicing the Spiritual Life

What are the conditions of guidance regarding God's moral will? The Scripture is our primary means of guidance. What are we to do and not do in relying on the Word for guidance?

_____

_____

_____

Seek guidance in Scripture for the decision you need to make. Direct answers may not be found for nonmoral personal decisions, but the truth of God's Word will apply to your need. Write out the passage that speaks to your heart about your decision.

_____

_____

_____

Prayer

I will hear Your Word, Lord; I will listen to the law of my God! Your Word will be very near me; it will be in my mouth and in my heart so I may obey it. "Teach me what I cannot see; if I have done wrong, I will not do so again." "I will hasten and not delay to obey your commands." I have declared this day, Lord, that You are my God, and I will walk in Your ways; I will keep Your decrees, commands, and laws, and I will obey You. (Isa. 1:10; Deut. 30:14 paraphrased; Job 34:32; Ps. 119:60 not paraphrased; Deut. 26:17 paraphrased)

Prayers, Praises, and Personal Notes

_____

_____

_____

Scripture Reading: Matthew 15:15-20; Ephesians 5:3-5

Practicing the Spiritual Life

In making decisions, we need to follow God's moral will. What makes us unclean? Where do immoral and evil thoughts come from?

_____

_____

_____

What moral decisions do you need to make in order to be freed from immoral thoughts and/or behaviors? Make a specific commitment to overcome those sins.

_____

_____

_____

Prayer

O Holy God, I will not be a false witness who speaks lies and sows discord among Christians. I will not be greedy and bring trouble to my family. I will not be perverse and stir up dissension or be a gossip who separates close friends. For it is Your will, God, that I should be sanctified; that I should avoid sexual immorality; that I should learn to control my own body in a way that is holy and honorable; and that in this matter I should not wrong others or take advantage of them. Lord, You will punish me for all such sins. For God, You did not call me to be impure, but to live a holy life. (Prov. 6:19 KJV; Prov. 15:27a; 16:28;1 Thess. 4:3-4, 6a-7 paraphrased)

Prayers, Praises, and Personal Notes

_____

_____

_____

WEEK TEN

Run a Disciplined Race

"Therefore, since we are surrounded
by such a great cloud of witnesses,
let us throw off everything that hinders
and the sin that so easily entangles,
and let us run with perseverance
the race marked out for us."

HEBREWS 12:1

For many years I walked for exercise. I thought my habit was so established I wouldn't break it. Then I had a change in jobs and schedule, and I began slacking off. The rhythm of my routine had been broken. I walked less and less, and then I stopped. After we moved, I vowed I'd start exercising again.

I'd rise in the morning with good intentions. As the day wore on, I'd keep promising myself that I'd walk in a few minutes—after I finished a certain job, before lunch, before dinner, then after dinner. I'd find excuses. It was too hot or too cold, or I was too tired or had too much work to do. By dark it was too late.

Then I prayed for and found a walking partner. Shirlee and I started walking four days a week, and my whole attitude changed. We walk half an hour, and I hardly notice my aches or the time passing because we're so busy talking. I'm grateful for Shirlee's encouragement and prayers, the accountability, and that I've gotten back into the discipline of exercising.

I need to do a lot of good things. I think about how important they are for my personal and spiritual well-being and what a difference they'd make in my life. Yet my wanting and my doing don't seem to match. Though I knew it before, I'm learning it again: We need the support of others to run a disciplined spiritual race. If we're going to lead a godly life, we need to be accountable to the Lord and other Christians.

Thinking that we need to be godly, vowing that we will be, and having good intentions don't make us holy. We may be committed to the Lord, determined that we need to grow spiritually, and make resolutions to become more godly and yet fail to reach our goal.[1] Being holy requires more than having the desire; we need to follow Jesus' example of what it means to lead a disciplined life.

The Disciplined Life of Christ

At first glance, it doesn't seem that Jesus led a disciplined life. He wandered from town to village, responding to the emergency of the moment as He taught the people, healed them, and delivered them from demons. He spontaneously met each need as it arose.

Once He went by boat to a remote place for a time of solitude, but the people He'd been ministering to followed Him on foot. When He reached shore and saw the large crowds, He had compassion on them and healed those who were sick. As evening approached, the disciples reminded Jesus that they had no food to feed 5,000 people (Matt. 14:13-15).

Jesus didn't teach the disciples how to prepare for such events. He didn't hold evangelism crusade strategy meetings with them. He simply and miraculously fed the people using five loaves of bread and two fishes.

He didn't fit the image of a leader driven to build His own empire. "On the contrary, everything we know about Jesus indicates that he was concerned with only one thing: to do the will of his Father. Nothing in the Gospels is as impressive as Jesus' single-minded obedience to his Father. From his first recorded words in the Temple, 'Did you not know that I must be busy with my Father's affairs?' (Luke 2:49), to his last words on the cross, 'Father, into your hands I commit my spirit' (Luke 23:46), Jesus' only concern was to do the will of his Father."[2]

Everywhere Jesus went, every miracle He performed, everything He ever did was done under the direction of His Father. "'I tell you the truth, the Son can do nothing by himself; he can do only what he sees his Father doing, because whatever the Father does the Son also does. For the Father loves the Son and shows him all he does,'" said Jesus (John 5:19-20a).

He did not lead a self-ordered life. "Jesus is not only our Savior simply because of what he said to us or did for us. He is our Savior because what he said and did was said and done in obedience to his Father."[3]

Jesus showed us through His single-minded obedience what it means to lead a holy, disciplined life. "His obedience means a total, fearless listening to his loving Father. Between the Father and the Son there is only love. . . . It is a caring, yet demanding love. It is a supportive, yet severe love. It is a gentle, yet strong love. It is a love that gives life, yet accepts death. In this divine love Jesus was sent into the world; to this divine love Jesus offered himself on the cross."[4]

He not only submitted Himself to the demands of love, but He also demonstrated what it means to be perfected in suffering. "Although he was a son, he learned obedience from what he suffered and, once made perfect, he became the source of eternal salvation for all who obey him" (Heb. 5:8-9).

Jesus demonstrated how we're to run the spiritually disciplined race. He did nothing by Himself, and neither can we. He did everything in accordance with His Father's will, and so must we. Jesus learned obedience through suffering, and so can we. As Jesus loved and obeyed His Father, so must we.

Submit to the Lord's Discipline

As I've worked on every chapter of this book, my willingness to be obedient and submit to the Lord's discipline has been tested. The validity of my faith in, commitment to, and love for the Lord have been challenged in the very areas I've been writing about. This chapter on running a disciplined race has been no exception.

In fact, I hit a wall, stumbled, and injured myself. I wondered if I could get up and finish the race. I was racing the clock, but I could hardly write a word for four weeks. The pressure was unrelenting because I was so close to my deadline.

A series of trials threw me off balance. I needed time to recover, but I knew I didn't have that luxury. The doctor was concerned that I had congestive heart failure, although it turned out later that I didn't. But the possibility terrified me. I had to take immediate medical measures.

I was also extremely fatigued despite being treated for sleep apnea. Then I came down with a painful bladder infection. I was seeing different doctors, having numerous medical tests, and went to the hospital for an all-night sleep study test. That night I only had four hours' sleep.

The next morning I drove three hours back home, praying that I'd make it safely since I was so exhausted. That evening I discovered that the technician who had reset my breathing machine had not put back an essential part into the carrying case, making the machine inoperable.

Sleep apnea can be life threatening, because the breathing passageway collapses frequently during sleep, causing partial or complete blockage and placing added stress on the heart. Until I could get the part for the machine, I'd have to sleep sitting up at night so I wouldn't stop breathing as often.

It was Friday night, and I had no idea how to obtain a part for the machine on the weekend. Fortunately, after several calls I reached the director of the sleep institute in Orange County. She arranged for a medical supply company in our area to make an emergency delivery of a new part on Saturday. I was grateful, but the ordeal and two nights without adequate sleep added to my exhaustion.

We also experienced a series of devastating crises among close friends and extended family members that deeply affected our lives. The heartache of those concerns increased the stress enormously.

In addition, not enough students enrolled in the vocational class I was team-teaching, so we closed it. I wouldn't have a paycheck for two months.

I was so consumed by these trials that I thought of nothing else. I had difficulty dealing with the shock of my physical problems and making the changes they required. The intense pressure was depleting my emotional reserves, taxing my mental concentration and physical energy, and testing me spiritually. I was anxious about everything and peaceful about nothing.

When I did have a block of free time, I used it unwisely. I escaped by watching television or preparing for a new English class scheduled for the following semester. I wasn't disciplining myself to do what I knew the Lord wanted me to do, which was to write this book.

I felt as if the Lord's timing was way off, and I was ready to drop out. How could I complete this book when I was in shock and struggling to survive the bombardment of trials? Yet the Lord always has a way of ministering to me and sending me exactly what I need at the perfect time. I read an article by a runner who compared a race he'd run with our spiritual life.

"As I ran my race, I saw others stop to walk or rest. Their lack of fitness and resolve had limited their efforts. Some of the runners walked a bit and then resumed. . . . But others who stopped to walk did not finish the race or complete it soon enough to pass the test. So it is in our service to the Lord. Some stop, finding the pace too difficult to maintain. They drop out of the race. Some return and finish, and some do not. . . . Let us strive to stay in the race. Or if we've dropped out, let us endeavor to run again while there is still time."[5]

I, too, was reminded of many Christians who had quit the race. Many dropped out because the pressure and the pain were more than they were willing to endure. Injuries caused by sin have knocked others out of the race.

If I genuinely desired to grow in godliness I had a choice. I could quit, or I could deal with my sins, endure the pain, resist the urge to drop out, release my hurts to the Lord, and finish the task. I realized that I needed to submit myself to the Lord's discipline and keep on running the race. Though I was having devotions, I still needed to spend more time spiritually nourishing myself in the Word and in prayer with others. It was the only way I was going to make it across the finish line. I was far too weak to run the race alone.

God was teaching me that at the center of a disciplined life is obedience. And at the center of genuine obedience is reverential fear, humble submission to, and unconditional love for our Lord—even in the midst of our most devastating circumstances and deepest heartaches.

"He has different ways of doing things, and we have to be trained and disciplined into His ways. It was said of Jesus—'He shall not fall nor be discouraged,' because He never worked from His own individual standpoint but always from the standpoint of His Father, and we have to learn to do the same."[6]

Though I was deeply discouraged, I knew I needed to see the onslaught of trials from the Lord's standpoint, not my own. As I spent more time with Him, refused to dwell on my pain, and forced myself to keep on running the spiritual race, I began to regain my strength and pick up the pace. When my grief, anxious feelings, and fears hit me full force, I kept fixing my thoughts on the Lord and His Word until they diminished.

I reaffirmed in my mind and heart that the Lord is always with me. The reality of my trials didn't change, but my thought life changed as I disciplined my mind by meditating on these passages: "You will keep in perfect peace all who trust in you, whose thoughts are fixed on you" (Isa. 26:3 NLT).

"Don't worry about anything; instead pray about everything. Tell God what you need, and thank him for all he has done. If you do this, you will experience God's peace, which is far more wonderful than the human mind can understand. His peace will guard your hearts and minds as you live in Christ Jesus. . . . Fix your thoughts on what is true and honorable and right. Think about things that are pure and lovely and admirable. Think about things that are excellent and worthy of praise" (Phil. 4:6-8b NLT).

By fixing my thoughts on the things that were true and right in my life, on the lovely and admirable blessings, I discovered the excellent things—my gratitude for a supportive praying husband, pastor, Christian friends, and church family. I praised the Lord for His providential leading and faithful provision.

Through Scripture, prayer, and accountability to other Christians and the Lord, He was training me to develop spiritual discipline. As I reflected on my more than forty-two years as a Christian, I realized how much the Lord loves me. Every trial and heartache that I've experienced, He has used for my highest spiritual good and redeemed for His greatest glory.

Train to Develop Spiritual Discipline

"Train yourself to be godly. For physical training is of some value, but godliness has value for all things, holding promise for both the present life and the life to come" (1 Tim. 4:7b-8). To reach the goal of spiritual maturity requires discipline and single-minded obedience.

Maintaining disciplined habits, however, hasn't been easy for me. Yet I'm continually learning that without them, I cannot run the kind of spiritual race that the Lord desires of me. Training develops discipline, discipline strengthens obedience, and obedience makes spiritual growth possible.

Here are some ways we may discipline ourselves to run this lifelong spiritual race.

We must train ourselves to be consistent. "Every Christian who makes progress in holiness is a person who has disciplined his life so that he spends regular time in the Bible. There is simply no other way."[7]

Daily we need to read, study, and reflect on the meaning of Scripture and apply it to our lives. As we go about our normal work, we need to meditate on verses and hymns that come to mind. We also need to memorize Scripture and faithfully listen to the Word as it's taught to us by pastors and Christian leaders.[8]

Participating in Bible Study Fellowship or Community Bible Study (interdenominational studies that may be offered in your area) is an excellent way to learn the Word of God and strengthen our walk with the Lord. Small group Bible studies are also a vital way to train ourselves spiritually.

Find running partners. Pray with one or two people on a regular basis. Judie and I meet once a week. One friend and I are not able to pray every week, but we pray as often as we can.

This pattern has worked well for us. We take turns discussing our needs and writing our requests in a small loose-leaf notebook. Sharing our burdens helps us gain spiritual insights, find balance, release our concerns, and pray more effectively. We also go over our requests from previous weeks and rejoice together about how God has specifically answered, which has been essential to building our faith and strengthening our prayer life.

As we run this spiritual race, we need encouragers who help us keep up the pace, whose example and support inspires us to continue running even when we don't feel we can put one foot in front of the other. It gives us strength to "know that we are not alone or forgotten as we run the race, especially when the stretch of road we are on grows long and lonely."[9]

Pace ourselves. This life is a distance marathon; it's not a one-mile race. "The best pace is the one that enables us to put forth our best effort yet finish the course without 'burning out' short of the goal. In other words, the right pace is challenging yet attainable!"[10]

Run our own course. We're not competing against anyone else. God has set the right course for us. Some Christians will run the spiritual race a lot faster than we will and others a lot slower. Cheer on those who pass us by and lovingly encourage those who lag behind.

Get back on track when we fall. As we train ourselves to be holy, we'll trip over obstacles and fall. Jerry Bridges said, "A verse of Scripture I often use in the face of failure with my own sins is Proverbs 24:16: 'For a righteous man falls seven times, and rises again, but the wicked stumble in time of calamity.'"

No matter how many times we fall and injure ourselves and others, we need to get up. We must continue to correct sins that cause us to stumble, rejoin the race, and keep running even when every part of us hurts and our pain is intolerable.[11]

Cross the finish line. The only way we can keep running until the race is over is to rely on the Holy Spirit's strength. "Finishing is its own reward: it is a time of well-earned rest! The pain stops, the breathing gets easier, and there is joy and camaraderie as the runners smile and pat each other on the back. Isn't that a preview of Heaven—when we will cross that final finish line and find real rest? Fellowship among those who have suffered together is the sweetest of all, and it awaits us there, along with the congratulations from those who have finished before us. What a joy and what a motivation it is to press on in our own race today!"[12]

When we cross that finish line, we'll experience an exhilarating, thrilling victory celebration that will continue throughout eternity!

Scripture Reading: John 5:19-21, 30; 8:27-29

Practicing the Spiritual Life

How did Jesus submit Himself to the discipline of doing His Father's will?

_____

_____

_____

In what areas of your life have you not yet submitted to the Lord to do His will?

_____

_____

_____

Prayer

Lord, I will find out what pleases You. I will obey Your commands, for I live in You, and You in me. And this is how I know that You live in me: I know it by Your Holy Spirit that You gave me. So I will make it my goal to please You. Apart from You I can do nothing. O God, deliver me from living the rest of my earthly life for evil human desires, but rather for Your will. For this world and its desires will pass away, but if I do Your will, I live forever. (Eph. 5:10; 1 John 3:24; 2 Cor. 5:9a; John 15:5b; 1 John 2:17 paraphrased)

Prayers, Praises, and Personal Notes

_____

_____

_____

_____

Scripture Reading: Hebrews 12:1-4

Practicing the Spiritual Life
In fixing our eyes on Jesus, what are we to consider?

_____

_____

_____

What is hindering you that you need to lay aside, and what sins are keeping you from running the spiritual race with perseverance?

_____

_____

_____

Prayer
Jesus, if I conceal my sins, I will not prosper; therefore, I will confess, throw off, and renounce my sins that I may find mercy, O Lord. "I am deeply sorry for what I have done." Forgive my sin once more, I pray. Since You have gone through suffering and temptation, You are able to help me when I am being tempted. And, as Your dear friend, who belongs to You and is bound for heaven, I will fix my thoughts on You, Jesus. I will not throw away my confident trust in You, no matter what happens. I will remember the great reward it brings me! Patient endurance and perseverance are what I need now, so I can continue to do Your will. Then I will receive all that you have promised. (Prov. 28:13 KJV paraphrased; Ps. 38:18b NLT not paraphrased; Ex. 10:17a; Heb. 2:18–3:1a NLT; 10:35-36 NLT paraphrased)

Prayers, Praises, and Personal Notes

_____

_____

_____

Scripture Reading: Hebrews 12:5-14

Practicing the Spiritual Life

Whom does the Lord discipline and for what reason? According to verses 12-14, how are we to respond to being disciplined?

_____

_____

_____

In what areas of your life do you still need to submit to the Lord's discipline?

_____

_____

_____

Prayer

Merciful and loving God, You disciplined me when I was unruly. Now restore me, and I will return to You, because You are the Lord my God. For I am happy and fortunate to be reproved by You; I will not despise nor reject Your correction and discipline. I will not lose heart, become discouraged, utterly spiritless, exhausted, and weary through fear. I will submit to You, Lord, and be at peace with You. I will make level paths for my feet and take only ways that are firm. For You are the Lord my God; I will consecrate myself to You and be holy, because You are holy. (Jer. 31:18b; Job 5:17 AMP; 2 Cor. 4:16a AMP; Job 22:21a; Prov. 4:26; Lev. 11:44a paraphrased)

Prayers, Praises, and Personal Notes

_____

_____

_____

_____

Scripture Reading: Proverbs 3:11-12; 5:11-14, 23

Practicing the Spiritual Life

What should our attitude be regarding the Lord's discipline? What will we realize at the end of our lives if we hate instruction?

_____

_____

_____

Do you feel resentment toward the Lord's discipline? If so, write a prayer asking the Lord to give you the attitude He desires.

_____

_____

_____

Prayer

God of Wisdom, I will listen to a life-giving rebuke so that I may be at home among the wise. For if I ignore discipline, I despise myself; therefore, I will heed correction and gain understanding. I will get the truth and will never sell it; I will also get wisdom, discipline, and discernment. I will listen to counsel, receive instruction, and accept correction that I may be wise. O Lord, "give me understanding and I will obey your law; I will put it into practice with all my heart." (Prov. 15:31-32; Prov. 23:23 NLT; Prov. 19:20a AMP paraphrased; Ps. 119:34 NLT not paraphrased)

Prayers, Praises, and Personal Notes

_____

_____

_____

_____

Scripture Reading: 1 Corinthians 9:24-27

Practicing the Spiritual Life

What are we running for, and how are we to run the spiritual race?

_____

_____

_____

What specific goal will you set for yourself this week to help you train for and run the spiritual race?

_____

_____

_____

Prayer

Master Coach, I will train myself toward godliness and keep myself spiritually fit. For physical training is of some value to me, but godliness and spiritual training is useful and of value in everything, for it holds promise for my present life and also for my life to come. I will consider my life worth nothing to me, if only I may finish the race and complete the task You have given me, Lord Jesus—the task of telling others the Good News of God's grace. I will press on toward the goal to win the prize for which You, Lord, have called me heavenward in Christ Jesus. (1 Tim. 4:7b-8 AMP; Acts 20:24; Phil. 3:14 paraphrased)

Prayers, Praises, and Personal Notes

_____

_____

_____

_____

Scripture Reading: 2 Timothy 4:6–8

Practicing the Spiritual Life

What did Paul do to lead a godly life? What is stored up for those who long for the Lord's appearing?

_____

_____

_____

How do you desire to cross the final finish line?

_____

_____

_____

Prayer

Almighty God, I will fight the good fight of faith. I will take hold of the eternal life to which I was called when I made my good confession of faith in the presence of many witnesses. I will let endurance, steadfastness, patience, and perseverance have full play and do a thorough work in my life, so that I may be mature and complete, lacking in nothing. I will keep hold of the deep truths of the faith with a clear conscience. Jesus, You are coming soon. Therefore, I will hold on to what I have, so that no one will take my crown. And when You appear, I will receive the crown of glory that will never fade away. (1 Tim. 6:12; James 1:4 AMP, NIV; 1 Tim. 3:9; Rev. 3:11; 1 Peter 5:4 paraphrased)

Prayers, Praises, and Personal Notes

_____

_____

_____

_____

Scripture Reading: Psalm 94:10-14

Practicing the Spiritual Life

What does the Lord do for and promise the person He disciplines?

_____

_____

_____

In what areas of your life do you need relief from trouble? What do you desire the Lord to teach you through discipline?

_____

_____

_____

Prayer

"Answer me when I call to you, O my righteous God. Give me relief from my distress; be merciful to me and hear my prayer." For, Lord, You love judgment and will not forsake me, Your saint; I am preserved forever, but the seed of the wicked shall be cut off. Now teach me to number my days aright that I may gain a heart of wisdom. I delight to do Your will, O my God; yes, Your law is within my heart. I will put my trust in You and will not forget Your deeds but will keep Your commands. "For these commands are a lamp, this teaching is a light, and the corrections of discipline are the way to life." (Ps. 4:1 not paraphrased; Ps. 37:28 KJV; Ps. 90:12; Ps. 40:8 KJV; Ps. 78:7 paraphrased; Prov. 6:23 not paraphrased)

Prayers, Praises, and Personal Notes

_____

_____

_____

_____

WEEK ELEVEN

Remember to Give the Gift of Grace

*"Each one should use whatever gift he has received
to serve others, faithfully administering
God's grace in its various forms."*

1 PETER 4:10

*G*ifts of grace are special remembrances given in a loving way and at a great sacrifice to the givers. Several years ago, I received two such gifts that especially touched my heart. One was a pair of black patent leather shoes with bows, the second, two purple ribbons.

At that time I was teaching English in southern California to immigrants from many parts of the world. They were attending twenty hours of intensive English classes per week. Most students had families to care for and worked at minimum wage or below in sweatshops, water-bottling factories, and other back-breaking jobs. Many of them lived with their families in a single rented room, sharing a communal kitchen and bathroom with other families. One man attended class all week even though he was living in his car with his wife, an infant, and two preschool daughters until the room he wanted to rent became available.

The students told me about their lives but not in a complaining way. They spoke about their desire to learn English quickly and work hard in order to make a better life for themselves and their children. I was amazed by their diligence despite their difficult lives.

Unmerited Acts of Kindness

Kenn was one of those students. Learning English was extremely hard for him, because he was illiterate in his own language. He always sat in a front seat, but I had a large class and was unable to give him much individual help. I often asked more advanced students to assist Kenn; however, they weren't able to help him since his ability to learn seemed limited. He didn't speak often, but when he did, most of us had difficulty understanding him.

At the end of the semester, he brought me an appreciation gift—a pair of black patent leather shoes with bows, in my exact size. I have no idea why Kenn gave me shoes or how he knew what size to buy. I wore the shoes at our closing class party. When I pointed to them and thanked Kenn, he didn't say a word but giggled with delight and embarrassment. I felt that I had not merited such a gift. Out of that classroom of students, I had helped him the least of all.

A couple years later, my students remembered me in a most gracious way. I was teaching my class when a secretary came to tell me that my father had passed away. I quickly excused the students and left.

The day of the funeral when my family and I arrived a few minutes before the service, a group of Vietnamese students dressed in black were standing in the lobby. They had arrived half an hour before and had been waiting for me. Each student shook my hand, offered sympathy, and then quietly left before the service.

When I went into the funeral chapel, I discovered an enormous floral wreath. Two purple ribbons were draped across the front, bearing the following words of condolence handwritten in silver: "With deeper sympathy; Vietnamese Students." I was greatly surprised by their generous remembrance and overcome by their expression of love in coming to the funeral home.

Sacrificial Gifts of Grace

Their generosity reminded me of the story Jesus told about the poor widow who put two copper coins into the temple treasury. He said, "All these people gave their gifts out of their wealth; but she out of her poverty put in all she had to live on" (Luke 21:4). Some of the poorest of this earth are the most gracious in giving.

What touched my heart was not the cost of the gifts but what they cost the givers. Their acts of kindness reminded me of what God gave me by His grace, at such a great sacrifice—the death of His only Son. Just as I could not give a material gift of equal value to thank my students, I cannot give Christ a gift of equal value in return.

He bestowed His favor upon me even though I didn't merit it. The kindest and only thing I could do for my students was to express my depth of gratitude to each one of them and continue to serve them as their teacher. In the same way, I can receive Jesus' gift of grace and sacrificial kindness to me with heartfelt thanksgiving and commit my life to Him in service.

Compassionate Grace

To lead holy lives, we need to show God's gracious love to others. We're called to demonstrate God's compassion to all people, not just those who meet our standard of acceptability. "This is what the Lord Almighty says: 'Administer true justice; show mercy and compassion to one another. Do not oppress the widow or the fatherless, the alien or the poor. In your hearts do not think evil of each other'" (Zech. 7:9-10).

God has called me to serve the poor. Now I am teaching English in mid-state California in a rural area. Most of the immigrants who attend my classes are field workers. Strawberries are one of the largest crops, and they are hand-picked. In the intense heat of the sun or in the rain, workers are stooped over rows of berries plucking that ripe, luscious fruit we enjoy without thought.

If you've ever tramped through a muddy field, your shoes sinking into the mire, you know how exhausting it can be after just a short walk. Imagine stooping all day long, slogging through the mud, coming home after ten or more hours of bone-wearying labor, showering, eating, and then going to class because you want to make a better life for yourself.

Recently, the students asked if we could discuss discrimination. I asked them to write their discussion questions on cards. One asked, "Why don't the field workers receive the best salary if the people that work in the fields work more than other workers?"

I could not answer that question. Immigrants—who are here illegally, legally, or have become United States citizens—experience appalling discrimination. Once I was blind to their needs, but God has opened my heart to their plight and given me the privilege of serving them.

Jeremiah said of King Josiah, "'He defended the cause of the poor and needy, and so all went well. Is that not what it means to know me?' declares the Lord" (Jer. 22:16). Genuine holiness calls us to demonstrate the Lord's grace and loving-kindness to the needy, because that's what it means to serve Him.

Humble Grace

God gives grace to the humble. "That is why Scripture says: 'God opposes the proud but gives grace to the humble.' Submit yourselves, then, to God. . . . Humble yourselves before the Lord, and he will lift you up" (James 4:6b-7a, 10).

"Pride is always there, ever ready to defend itself. It is also clever. It has the ability to go underground and mask its ugliness in subtle, quiet ways. Because it doesn't fit the Christian life for anyone to be overtly proud, we find our pride in other ways: our work, our salaries, our prestige, the power and influence we wield, our titles, our clothing, our approach to people, our tendency to manipulate. . . . As powerful as any influence, pride is a classic grace killer."[1]

Pride is also a classic people killer. The proud feel superior at the expense of another person's dignity and humanity. Pride is prejudice. And prejudice demeans, devalues, and discriminates against others.

Holiness calls us to serve one another with tender, humble compassion. "Do not be proud, but be willing to associate with people of low position. Do not be conceited" (Rom. 12:16b). "Finally, all of you, live in harmony with one another; be sympathetic, love as brothers, be compassionate and humble" (1 Peter 3:8).

Some of the poorest and most unpretentious people have greatly ministered to me and others. A young man in one of my vocational classes was a migrant farm worker who worked long, back-breaking hours. He had a sleeping bag for a bed, an old car, and few other possessions. Yet he constantly helped other students. I don't speak Spanish, so he translated for the other students and helped them with their textbook assignments. He didn't ask if he could help; he simply gave himself to others wherever he saw a need.

A woman I once knew was a humble, unpretentious person who had a very hard life. She'd had polio as a child and often suffered crippling pain from the aftereffects. She was a great pray-er. When she interceded for others, God answered. She had an uncanny sense of knowing when others needed prayer and would call them.

Although I didn't know it until later, when my husband had heart surgery, she had prayed that God would send many people to be with me and comfort me during the operation. It wasn't until I told her how amazed I was that seventeen people had waited with me the day of the surgery that she told me what she had prayed for me.

Sacrificial Grace

Holiness calls us to excel in sacrificial giving. Paul commended the Macedonian churches for their giving. "Out of the most severe trial, their overflowing joy and their extreme poverty welled up in rich generosity. For I testify that they gave as much as they were able, and even beyond their ability" (2 Cor. 8:2-3a). Then Paul urged the Corinthians to follow the same example. "But just as you excel in everything—in faith, in speech, in knowledge, in complete earnestness and in your love for us—see that you also excel in this grace of giving" (2 Cor. 8:7).

My husband's parents were an example throughout their lives of sacrificial giving. They had a small home and a below-average income. Yet if there was a need, they gave clothes, food, and money to single mothers, widows, the unemployed, and the poor. They tithed faithfully to their church and sent offerings to missionaries. They gave far more than they could afford, but they never went without.

When my mother-in-law, who had Alzheimer's disease, went into a convalescent home, she was greatly loved and cared for by the nurses. Since we lived 1,500 miles away, her friend Marion voluntarily and faithfully visited her and advised us of my mother-in-law's needs the entire eight years she was in the home.

Ron's parents had helped Marion when she was widowed, and she remembered their kindness. By God's tender grace, my mother-in-law was cared for in the same way she had given to others.

We may help others in many practical ways and, in doing so, encourage them in their faith. Ron has taken clothes to a Christian rehabilitation home for former prisoners. Prison chaplains always need Bibles and literature to give to inmates. Missionaries not only need faithful financial support, but they often need cars, clothing, furnishings, and help in finding housing when they come home on furlough. Our church has a closet filled with practical items for returning missionaries.

Give clothing and furniture for infants and children to families in your church. Gather several people together and spend a few hours making meals, cleaning house, and doing laundry for someone who is seriously ill. My friend Doris adopts women in convalescent homes, visits them regularly, takes them teddy bears and other small gifts, and regularly prays for and with them.

Those are only a few ways we may meet people's needs. Prayer is one of the most vital ways and should not be underestimated. But at the same time saying, "I will pray for you," may be an excuse for not showing kindness in a tangible way.

Jesus showed us how we are to follow His gracious, humble ways. He was a caring servant to the hungry, helpless, needy, and poor. He left us a pattern to follow, and when He returns, our inheritance will be based on what we did for those in the greatest need.

When we feed the hungry, we are feeding Christ. When we give water to the thirsty, we are giving Christ a drink. When we invite strangers into our churches and homes, we are inviting Christ. When we give clothes to those who need them, we are clothing Jesus; when we care for the sick, we are caring for Him; when we visit those in prison, we are visiting Him (Matt. 25:34-37). When we do these acts with loving-kindness, we are giving grace and living grace.

Scripture Reading: Deuteronomy 15:7-11

Practicing the Spiritual Life

What kind of heart are we to have toward the poor and needy, and how are we to care for them? What will God do for us when we give to others with a generous heart?

_____

_____

_____

Ask the Lord to show you someone with a specific need and how you can meet that need in a compassionate, sensitive, and caring way. Make a commitment to do the act of kindness by a certain time.

_____

_____

_____

Prayer

Lord, I have freely received; therefore, I will freely give. I will open my hands to the poor; yes, I will reach out to the needy with my hands filled. Then I will know the blessing of generously sharing my food with the poor. By being generous, my soul will prosper and be enriched; when I refresh others, I will myself be refreshed. (Matt. 10:8b; Prov. 31:20 AMP; Prov. 22:9; 11:25 paraphrased)

Prayers, Praises, and Personal Notes

_____

_____

_____

_____

Scripture Reading: 2 Chronicles 28:1-15

Practicing the Spiritual Life

Why did Oded, the prophet, and the other leaders intervene for the prisoners? What did they do to take care of the prisoners' needs?

_____

_____

_____

Pray today for Christians suffering unjustly around the world. Is there anything you can do about an unjust situation? If so, what?

_____

_____

_____

Prayer

"My whole being will exclaim, 'Who is like you, O Lord? You rescue the poor from those too strong for them, the poor and needy from those who rob them.'" You uphold the cause of the oppressed and give food to the hungry. You, Lord, set prisoners free. Therefore, I will not exploit the poor, because they are poor and will not crush the needy in court. Yes, I will speak up for the poor and helpless and see that they get justice. (Ps. 35:10 not paraphrased; Ps. 146:7; Prov. 22:22; Prov. 31:9 NLT paraphrased)

Prayers, Praises, and Personal Notes

_____

_____

_____

_____

_____

Scripture Reading: Matthew 25:31-46

Practicing the Spiritual Life

How does Jesus contrast the difference between those who care for the needy and those who give nothing? When we give to the poor, to whom are we giving?

_____

_____

_____

How did this passage speak to your heart about caring for those in need as Jesus would have you do?

_____

_____

_____

Prayer

Lord, the kind of fast You have chosen is not just a day for me to humble myself. The kind of fasting You have chosen for me is to loose the chains of injustice and untie the cords of the yoke, to set the oppressed free and break every yoke. It is to share my food with the hungry and to provide the poor wanderer with shelter—when I see the naked, to clothe them, and not to turn away from my own flesh and blood. And if I spend myself in behalf of the hungry and satisfy the needs of the oppressed, then my light will rise in the darkness, and my night will become like the noonday. (Isa. 58:5a, 6-7, 10 paraphrased)

Prayers, Praises, and Personal Notes

_____

_____

_____

Scripture Reading: Mark 12:41-44

Practicing the Spiritual Life

What comparison did Jesus make between what the rich people and the widow gave to the treasury?

_____

_____

_____

How do you believe Jesus would have you give to the church and other ministries?

_____

_____

_____

Prayer

O generous and ever-giving God, a little that a righteous person has is better than the riches of many wicked. Therefore, I will be among the righteous who show mercy and give generously. Out of the most severe trial, I will overflow with joy, and in extreme poverty I will well up in rich generosity. I will give as much as I am able, and even beyond my ability. I will give, and it shall be given unto me; good measure, pressed down, and shaken together, and running over, shall others give to me. For with the same measure that I use when I give to others shall be measured to me again. (Ps. 37:16, 21b KJV; 2 Cor. 8:2-3; Luke 6:38 KJV paraphrased)

Prayers, Praises, and Personal Notes

_____

_____

_____

Scripture Reading: Acts 9:36-42

Practicing the Spiritual Life

How did Dorcas bless people in a special way? How did the Lord use the miracle in this passage?

_____

_____

_____

What are some things you can do or make in order to give to those in need?

_____

_____

_____

Prayer

Ever kind and giving Lord, teach me how to use whatever gift I have received to serve others, faithfully administering Your grace in its various forms. Then I will do good deeds, as one who has brought up children, who has practiced hospitality to strangers, who has washed the feet of the saints, who has helped to relieve the distressed, and devoted myself to doing good in every way. I will also consider how I may spur others on toward love and good deeds. I will let my light so shine before others that they may see my good works and glorify You, Father, who are in heaven. (1 Peter 4:10; 1 Tim. 5:10 AMP; Heb. 10:24; Matt. 5:16 KJV paraphrased)

Prayers, Praises, and Personal Notes

_____

_____

_____

_____

Scripture Reading: 2 Corinthians 9:6-15

Practicing the Spiritual Life

How are we to give, sow, and serve?

_____

_____

_____

Set specific goals to increase in giving and serving Christ. Set a goal for this week, month, and year.

_____

_____

_____

Prayer

Lord, I will honor You with my income and with the first fruits of all my labor. For You commanded me to do good, to be rich in good deeds, and to be generous and willing to share. By Your grace and my own hard work, I will help the weak, remembering Your very words, Lord Jesus: "It is more blessed to give than to receive." Strengthen me so that I will not grow weary in doing good, for at the proper time I will reap a harvest if I do not give up. Therefore, as I have opportunity, I will do good to all people, especially to those who belong to the family of believers. (Prov. 3:9; 1 Tim. 6:18; Acts 20:35 not paraphrased; Gal. 6:9-10 paraphrased)

Prayers, Praises, and Personal Notes

_____

_____

_____

_____

Scripture Reading: Romans 16:1-16; 2 Timothy 1:15-18

Practicing the Spiritual Life

In what ways did Christians minister the gift of grace to Paul and to the churches? What did Onesiphorus especially do for Paul?

_____

_____

_____

In these passages we see how God used many ordinary people to serve. What gifts of grace can you use to serve the church and others?

_____

_____

_____

Prayer

Lord Jesus, the gifts You have given us are different, according to the grace you have given. If my gift is prophesying, may I use it in proportion to my faith. If it is serving, may I serve; if it is teaching, may I teach; if it is encouraging, may I encourage; if it is contributing to the needs of others, may I give generously; if it is leadership, may I govern diligently; if it is showing mercy, may I do it cheerfully. By Your grace, Lord, I will be devoted to others in love. I will honor others above myself. I will never be lacking in zeal, but keep my spiritual fervor, serving You, Lord. I will share with God's people who are in need and practice hospitality. (Rom. 12:6-8, 10-11, 13 paraphrased)

Prayers, Praises, and Personal Notes

_____

_____

_____

WEEK TWELVE

*Rejoice in
the Lord Always*

*"Glory in his holy name;
let the hearts of those who
seek the Lord rejoice."*

1 Chronicles 16:10

*T*he sunset cast a fiery glow across the crystal-blue sky. Clouds quilted in patches of apricot, rose, gray, and salmon-pink shone like satin. Vivid white light broke through in places. Below, the Pacific Ocean was a sea of glass—a glistening sheen on its vast mirrored surface. Beyond the horizon of distant islands, a half-circle sun shone its fire-orange light, pure and radiant. I was transfixed by the sun, which looked like a crown with shimmering rays of amber-yellow light streaming out from it. The luminous beams fanning out into the sky seemed to touch the edge of heaven.

I felt as if I'd glimpsed God's glory. That iridescent crown of light reminded me of the apostle John's vision recorded in Revelation. "And I saw what looked like a sea of glass mixed with fire and, standing beside the sea, those who had been victorious over the beast and his image and over the number of his name. They held harps given them by God and sang the song of Moses the servant of God and the song of the Lamb: 'Great and marvelous are your deeds, Lord God Almighty. Just and true are your ways, King of the ages. Who will not fear you, O Lord, and bring glory to your name? For you alone are holy'" (Rev. 15:2-4a).

What a magnificent sight that will be when His victorious saints sing to the glory of their God triumphant. What a day that will be when we join that vast sea of Christians in songs of praise, purified at last from all our sins, our joy heightened by the trials through which we have passed, and our holiness finally perfect. Even greater will be the indescribable joy of worshiping our glorious Savior in ecstasy beyond our ability to imagine.

Standing in God's Holy Presence

Seeing that crown of light was a divinely appointed moment for me. I was driving down the highway, and I kept trying to find a place to pull over, but when I finally found a place, the golden crown had slipped behind the island. Though I spent a few minutes worshiping God and watching the waning sunset, I was weighed down by the concerns of my heart.

Rejoicing in the Lord, praising, and worshiping Him is the weakest area of my spiritual life. I spend seconds rejoicing, compared to hours of praying for personal needs. I realize that I am hardly different from any other Christian, whose prayer life is centered on self and loved ones and the worries of life. Rejoicing is difficult for me when so many things are going wrong.

I've examined my own lack of thankfulness and seen what keeps me from rejoicing in the Lord—pride, grief over unanswered prayers, dissatisfaction with an answer when it does come, and always wanting more from God. I'm quick to beg and slow to praise.

Moreover, I am reluctant to worship God because when I do, I am overwhelmed by my own unworthiness, by feelings of guilt and shame, and by my mental battle with evil thoughts. I sometimes withdraw instead of dealing with the feelings and sins that hinder me from being drawn into the presence of a holy God, who seems to ask far more of me than I can ever be.[1]

Though we won't become perfectly holy in this life, worship is essential to growing in godliness. "God spoke, saying, 'Be ye holy; for I am holy.' He did not say 'Be ye as holy as I am holy,' for that would be to demand of us absolute holiness, something that belongs to God alone. Before the uncreated fire of God's holiness angels veil their faces. . . . No honest man can say, 'I am holy.'"[2]

"From one standpoint, you are exactly right if you feel that you're too sinful to stand in the presence of God and worship. But let our worship 'in Christ' in 'the beauty of His holiness'—remind us how His cleansing blood has touched us. Not only our tongues but our whole being—'washed in the blood of the lamb'!

"It is overwhelming to reflect on our sinfulness before a sinless God, but let us recognize with equal impact that through Christ we have been cleansed, enabled through no righteousness of our own, to stand before the holy God."[3]

It's not only sin that keeps us from worshiping our holy God, but we need to learn how to praise Him for who He is, not for what He will do for us. The questions we need to answer for ourselves are: Why, how, and for what do we worship the Lord? Once we know how to worship God, may we glorify Him with lips that sing hymns and songs of praise, with hearts that rejoice in Him, and lives that glorify His name.

Worship Father, Son, and Holy Spirit

"Come, let us bow down in worship, let us kneel before the Lord our Maker" (Ps. 95:6). Let us humble ourselves before the One who created us. Worship Him with gratitude and gladness.

As we worship the Father, Son, and Holy Spirit, persevering by faith and ever-increasing love, how do we discover the secret of being responsive to the moving of the Holy Spirit in our lives and to the transforming power of Christ to change us into His likeness? The answer to that secret "is simply the old and ever-new counsel: *Acquaint thyself with God.*"[4]

"To know God is at once the easiest and most difficult thing in the world. It is easy because the knowledge is not won by hard mental toil, but is something freely given. As sunlight falls free on the open field, so the knowledge of the holy God is a free gift to men who are open to receive it. But this knowledge is difficult because there are conditions to be met and the obstinate nature of fallen man does not take kindly to them."[5]

We acquaint ourselves with God through reading and applying Scripture to our lives, constantly praying, confessing and repenting of our sins, and praising Him for how He works in our lives, others' lives, and the church. We come to know Him as we worship and love Him more and more.

Rejoice in the Lord

"Rejoice in the Lord always. I will say it again: Rejoice!" (Phil. 4:4). "Joy is the soul of praise. To delight ourselves in God is most truly to extol him. . . . That God is, and that he is such a God, and our God, ours for ever and ever, should wake within us an unceasing and overflowing joy. To rejoice in temporal comforts is dangerous, to rejoice in self is foolish, to rejoice in sin is fatal, but to rejoice in God is heavenly."[6]

Rejoice in the Lord constantly, daily, always, and forevermore; join the universe in rejoicing that Christians around the world are proclaiming that Jesus is Savior and Lord. "Let the heavens rejoice, let the earth be glad; let them say among the nations, 'The Lord reigns!'" (1 Chron. 16:31).

Rejoice in the Lord when those who are lost are found and saved, when sinners repent, and for our own salvation, and that our names are written in heaven (Luke 10:20; 15:4-10).

Proclaim God's Sovereignty

"I will come and proclaim your mighty acts, O Sovereign Lord; I will proclaim your righteousness, yours alone" (Ps. 71:16). "God's sovereignty is the attribute by which He rules His entire creation, and to be sovereign, God must be all-knowing, all-powerful, and absolutely free. The reasons are these:

"Were even one datum of knowledge, however small, unknown to God, His rule would break down at that point. To be Lord over all the creation, He must possess all knowledge. And were God lacking one infinitesimal modicum of power, that lack would end His reign and undo His kingdom; that one stray atom of power would belong to someone else, and God would be a limited ruler and hence not sovereign."[7]

"The light of nature shows that there is a God, who has lordship and sovereignty over all; is good, and does good unto all; and is therefore to be feared, loved, praised, called upon, trusted in, and served, with all the heart, and with all the soul, and with all the might. But the acceptable way of worshiping the true God is instituted by himself, and so limited by his own revealed will, that he may not be worshiped according to the imaginations and devices of men, or the suggestions of Satan, under any visible representation, or any other way not prescribed in the holy Scripture."[8]

Proclaim God's sovereignty, worshiping Him in Spirit and in truth and according to God's Word (John 4:24). We must be careful that we're not deluded by the imaginations of the deceived or the Deceiver. Many new methods for "worshiping God" are actually guides for self-worship and self-affirmation, for lifting our self-esteem and praising ourselves.

Seeking to know ourselves, satisfying our own needs, striving for success and status, and becoming famous for doing evil more than for doing good have become the gods our society holds as sovereign today. A criminal receives more glory than a saint.

We have eternal glory to look forward to, so express gratitude for our Savior's sovereign reign over our lives, that He knows every intimate detail about us, that His all-powerful love controls everything that touches our lives.

Glory in His Holy Name

"Ascribe to the Lord the glory due his name; worship the Lord in the splendor of his holiness" (Ps. 29:2). Glory belongs to the Lord God alone, not to angels or to any human beings whom this world worships for their beauty and fame. Glory in His holy name, and give God the honor due Him. Glorify God for the magnificence of His beauty, power, and the brightness and splendor of His holiness.

Meditate on the names of God, for they reveal His nature, His promises, and His personal relationship with us. Exalt Almighty God, for none is mightier than He. Extol the Maker of heaven and earth, for He created and governs the vast galaxies of the universe. Hail the Alpha and Omega, the First and Last. Magnify the Everlasting Father who reigns on high.

Be thankful to the Shepherd and Overseer of our souls for watching over us. Love Jesus with the adoration of a little child. Honor the Crucified One for dying for our sins. Give glory to our Blessed Redeemer, who is our one and only Savior.

Express gratitude to the God of grace and mercy, who delivers us from evil. Offer sacrifices of thanksgiving to the Holy Comforter, Consoler, and Counselor, who bears our sorrows and hears our every cry.

Bow down before the great I AM WHO I AM. Praise the King of kings and Lord of lords. Sing to the Bright Morning Star, Master of everything, Rock of all ages. Shout for joy to our wonderful Lord. Worship Father, Son, and Holy Spirit. Sing hallelujah to Jesus Christ, the Lamb!

Offer to God a Sacrifice of Praise and Thanksgiving

"Through Jesus, therefore, let us continually offer to God a sacrifice of praise—the fruit of lips that confess his name" (Heb. 13:15). Be thankful that the Lord knows and cares that our praises are often a sacrifice. We may grieve over heartaches and at the same time express gratitude for God's presence and provision.

Praise Him for the privilege of entering into His afflictions. "But rejoice that you participate in the sufferings of Christ, so that you may be overjoyed when his glory is revealed" (1 Peter 4:13).

God never expects us to praise Him *for* the evil, injustice, or wrongdoing that afflicts us. What He desires from us is a sacrifice of thanksgiving for His loving presence and guiding hand that leads us through these trials. He knows our losses and desires to comfort and be with us in the valley of sorrow. Do we not feel the hurts of those we love more deeply than those of strangers? God even more feels the pain of those who are His, who are His very own beloved ones.

When we accuse God of abandoning us, we separate ourselves from His ever-caring presence. He has not left us, but we have turned away from Him. When we blame God, we deepen our pain.

When we thank the Lord sacrificially, no matter how artificial or insincere we may feel, He will lift us up and fill our hearts with peace and joy that will sustain us through the worst imaginable. Praise Him for His love and that He sees our afflictions and knows the anguish of our souls (Ps. 31:7). Thank Him that He alone is our refuge (Ps. 64:10).

"Let the sacrifice be really presented to the God who sees the heart, pay to him the love you promised, the service you covenanted to render, the loyalty of heart you have vowed to maintain. Oh for grace to do this! Oh that we may be graciously enabled to love God and live up to our profession! To be, indeed, the servants of the Lord, the lovers of Jesus—this is our main concern."[9]

Sing to the Lord Songs of Praise and Worship

"Sing to the Lord, you saints of his; praise his holy name" (Ps. 30:4). Singing hymns lifts our hearts into the very presence of God and causes us to forget self. The highest and most sacred means of worshiping God is in song. It thrills our hearts, causes us to weep with joy, and fills our soul with the glory of God.

Expressing "praise by sacred song is one of our greatest delights. We were created for this purpose, and hence it is a joy to us. It is a charming duty to praise the lovely name of our God.

"All pleasure is to be found in the joyful worship of Jehovah; all joys are in his sacred name, as perfumes lie slumbering in a garden of flowers. The mind expands, the soul is lifted up, the heart warms, the whole being is filled with delight when we are engaged in singing the high praises of our Father, Redeemer, Comforter."[10]

Praise the Lord

"I will praise thee, O Lord, with my whole heart; I will shew forth all thy marvellous works" (Ps. 9:1 KJV). "Gratitude for one mercy refreshes the memory as to thousands of others. One silver link in the chain draws up a long series of tender remembrances. Here is eternal work for us, for there can be no end to the showing forth of all his deeds of love."[11]

Praise the Lord for the great things He has done for us and for His abundant provisions. But we must be careful not to be proud in our praises, using them as a excuse to brag, or we'll discourage others in their faith. Watch that we do not use praise as a way to deceive ourselves that all is well when everything is wrong or to try to manipulate God to answer prayer.

Pure praise is free of pride or expectation. Praise offered by a humble heart encourages others in their faith and gives them hope that God is more than able to meet their greatest needs.

Keep a journal of answered prayer, of the Lord's mercies in times of heartache. Read over the journal and use it as a means to praise God for all that He has done and for His wonderful love and faithfulness. We need memorials of God's goodness to us, for it is far easier to remember our sorrows and trials.

"Praise the Lord. Do it again; continue to do it; do it better and more heartily; do it in growing numbers; do it at once. There are good reasons for praising the Lord, and among the first is this—for the Lord is good. He is so good that there is none good in the same sense or degree. He is so good that all good is found in him, flows from him, and is rewarded by him."[12]

I was reminded of God's goodness again this morning at sunrise. Yesterday it was dark and overcast. Throughout the night rains flooded the earth. Now at daybreak the sun is a round globe of bright-white light, its brilliancy so blinding I can only look upon it a few seconds. Beams of light radiating from around the white sun stream through the clouds.

With the wonder of a child, I watch the gray cumulus clouds tinged in cotton-white as they slowly float across the pure blue sky. The sun casts a soft white glow across the winter sky and on the water-laden earth. Glistening drops of water that look like crystal-clear Christmas lights dangle from the branch tips of the sequoia pines.

My focus is lifted beyond the confines of this earth to the highest heavens, to God who orchestrates radiant white sunrises and glorious fiery sunsets.

"From the rising of the sun to the place where it sets, the name of the Lord is to be praised." "The heavens praise your wonders, O Lord, your faithfulness too, in the assembly of the holy ones." "Praise the Lord. Praise the Lord from the heavens, praise him in the heights above." "Praise him, sun and moon, praise him, all you shining stars." "Praise him, you highest heavens and you waters above the skies." "Praise the Lord, O my soul. O Lord my God, you are very great; you are clothed with splendor and majesty" (Ps. 113:3; 89:5; 148:1, 3, 4; 104:1).

Scripture Reading: Matthew 4:1-11

Practicing the Spiritual Life

How did Satan tempt Jesus in regard to worship? What did Jesus say in response?

_____

_____

_____

What worldly temptations are you experiencing that keep you from worshiping the Lord? Worship the Lord by writing a letter expressing your love to Him.

_____

_____

_____

Prayer

"'Who will not fear you, O Lord, and bring glory to your name? For you alone are holy. All nations will come and worship before you, for your righteous acts have been revealed.'" I will worship You, Son of God, in the splendor of Your holiness; may all the earth tremble before You. I worship You with gladness and come before You with joyful songs. Since I am receiving a kingdom that cannot be shaken, I will be thankful, and so worship You, God, acceptably with reverence and awe. (Rev. 15:4 not paraphrased; Ps. 96:9; 100:2; Heb. 12:28 paraphrased)

Prayers, Praises, and Personal Notes

_____

_____

_____

Scripture Reading: Luke 15:4-10

Practicing the Spiritual Life
What causes great rejoicing in heaven?

_____

_____

_____

For what lost persons have you been praying? Write a prayer of rejoicing that the Lord is seeking those who are lost.

_____

_____

_____

Prayer
Lord, I will rejoice in You; I will be joyful in You, God my Savior. I will seek You and rejoice and be glad in You; I love Your salvation and will always say, "Lord, be exalted!" Surely You have granted me eternal blessings and made me glad with the joy of Your presence. "You have made known to me the path of life; you will fill me with joy in your presence, with eternal pleasures at your right hand." (Hab. 3:18; Ps. 40:16; 21:6 paraphrased; Ps. 16:11 not paraphrased)

Prayers, Praises, and Personal Notes

_____

_____

_____

_____

_____

Scripture Reading: Daniel 7:13-28

Practicing the Spiritual Life

What is the extent of God's sovereignty and power?

_____

_____

_____

By God's sovereign power, what will the saints be given? How does this promise give you hope regarding your eternal future? Record your gratitude for God's sovereign reign.

_____

_____

_____

Prayer

Bless the Lord, all His works in all places of His sovereign dominion; bless the Lord, O my soul. Dominion and awe belong to You, O God; You establish order in the heights of heaven. You shall have dominion from sea to sea, and from the river unto the ends of the earth. How great are Your signs! How mighty are Your wonders! Your kingdom is an everlasting kingdom, O sovereign God, and Your dominion is from generation to generation. (Ps. 103:22 KJV; Job 25:2; Ps. 72:8; Dan. 4:3 KJV paraphrased)

Prayers, Praises, and Personal Notes

_____

_____

_____

_____

_____

Scripture Reading: Psalm 72:17-19; Luke 24:36-47

Practicing the Spiritual Life

What do these passages say about the glory given God's name and the ministry that will be done in Jesus' name?

_____

_____

_____

Write a psalm of praise glorifying God's name.

_____

_____

_____

Prayer

"O Lord, our Lord, how majestic is your name in all the earth! You have set your glory above the heavens." I will glory in Your holy name; my heart seeks You, Lord, and rejoices. I will sing to the glory of Your name; I will make Your praise glorious! "Who will not fear you, O Lord, and bring glory to your name? For you alone are holy. All nations will come and worship before you, for your righteous acts have been revealed." Blessed are You, King Jesus, who comes in the name of the Lord; peace in heaven, and glory in the highest! (Ps. 8:1 not paraphrased; 1 Chron. 16:10; Ps. 66:2 paraphrased; Rev. 15:4 not paraphrased; Luke 19:38 KJV paraphrased)

Prayers, Praises, and Personal Notes

_____

_____

_____

Scripture Reading: Philippians 2:17-18; 2 Corinthians 6:4-10

Practicing the Spiritual Life

How did Paul respond when he suffered severe trials?

_____

_____

_____

For what heartaches and trials can you offer to the Lord a sacrifice of praise—for His presence with you in the troubles?

_____

_____

_____

Prayer

Lord Jesus, I will sacrifice a thank offering to You and call on Your name. Through You I will offer a sacrifice of praise to God continually, that is, the fruit of my lips giving thanks to Your name. I will sacrifice a freewill offering to You, Lord; I will praise Your name, for it is good. For You have delivered me from all my troubles. I will offer the sacrifices of thanksgiving and rehearse Your deeds with shouts of joy and singing! (Ps. 116:17; Heb. 13:15 KJV; Ps. 54:6-7a; Ps. 107:22 AMP paraphrased)

Prayers, Praises, and Personal Notes

_____

_____

_____

_____

_____

Scripture Reading: Psalm 149:1-5; Psalm 150

Practicing the Spiritual Life

In what ways are we to praise the Lord in song?

_____

_____

_____

Worship the Lord with hymns and songs of praise; focus your thoughts on the Lord as you sing. Record how the Lord spoke to your heart while you were praising Him.

_____

_____

_____

Prayer

Sweet Holy Spirit, I will praise Your name in song and glorify You with thanksgiving. I will give thanks to You because of Your righteousness and will sing praise to Your name. "I will be glad and rejoice in you; I will sing praise to your name, O Most High." I will sing to the glory of Your name; I will make Your praise glorious! "Praise the Lord. Praise the Lord, O my soul. I will praise the Lord all my life; I will sing praise to my God as long as I live." (Ps. 69:30; 7:17a paraphrased; Ps. 9:2 not paraphrased; Ps. 66:2 paraphrased; Ps. 146:1-2 not paraphrased)

Prayers, Praises, and Personal Notes

_____

_____

_____

_____

Scripture Reading: Psalm 148

Practicing the Spiritual Life

For what do all the angels, the heavenly hosts, and all creation praise the Lord?

_____

_____

_____

Pray and ask the Lord to bring praises to your heart and mind. Record them quickly as they come to you. Begin a memorial book of praise and worship.

_____

_____

_____

Prayer

"Praise the Lord, O my soul; all my inmost being, praise his holy name. Praise the Lord, O my soul, and forget not all his benefits." "I will praise you, O Lord, with all my heart; I will tell of all your wonders." I will bless You at all times: Your praise shall continually be in my mouth. "I will praise you forever for what you have done; in your name I will hope, for your name is good. I will praise you in the presence of your saints." "Every day I will praise you and extol your name for ever and ever." (Ps. 103:1-2; 9:1 not paraphrased; Ps. 34:1 KJV paraphrased; Ps. 52:9; 145:2 not paraphrased)

Prayers, Praises, and Personal Notes

_____

_____

_____

_____

_____

WEEK THIRTEEN

*Refresh Your Thirst
for Holiness*

*"Jesus declared, 'I am the bread of life.
He who comes to me will never go hungry,
and he who believes in me will never be thirsty.'"*

JOHN 6:35

SPIRITUAL RETREAT GUIDE

*I*n this special time set aside for seeking God, read the hymns and Scripture passages slowly; reflect on how the words relate to your own life and spiritual needs. Ask the Holy Spirit to refresh your thirst for holiness and transform your life as you are praying, reading the selections, and writing your responses. Respond to Him with an open heart and open mind.

When your thoughts wander, go back and read the hymns or Scriptures again. Ask the Lord to help you focus on the meaning of the passages and to listen with purity of heart and thought.

Write verses that especially speak to you on index cards (include the date). Later, when you reread those Scriptures and your retreat notes, you may find that they prepared you for an answer to prayer and showed how God would work.

Prepare for the Retreat

Date _____

Write down any needs, obligations, or worries that are concerning you now. Take a few moments to release them to the Lord.

_____

_____

_____

_____

In what ways would you like your spiritual thirst to be refreshed during this time with the Lord?

_____

_____

_____

Morning Quiet Time

"'Consecrate yourselves and be holy,
because I am the Lord your God.'"

LEVITICUS 20:7

Recreation *(10 to 20 minutes)*

Walk slowly and release your concerns to the Lord. You may want to write the above passage on an index card. As you walk, carry the card, read and reflect on the verse, praying that the Lord will refresh your thirst for holiness. As the Holy Spirit speaks to you, keep praying that you will be able to hear and respond and that He will enable you to change your heart, thoughts, and life.

Read and Respond

Find a quiet place for your time with the Lord. Write your responses as you feel the need and after any of the following "Scripture Readings," "Hymns to Sing or Reflect On," and "Quiet Listening."

Scripture Reading: John 4:1-30

Practicing the Spiritual Life

What kind of water did Jesus offer the Samaritan woman to quench her thirst?

_____

_____

When Jesus said that He was the Messiah, what did the woman do?

_____

_____

How are we to worship God?

_____

_____

_____

If Jesus met you during your daily routine, what might He say to you? How would you respond?

_____

_____

_____

Hymn to Sing or Reflect On

HOLY GHOST, LIGHT DIVINE

1. Holy Ghost, with light divine, Shine upon this heart of mine;
Chase the shades of night away, Turn my darkness into day.

2. Holy Ghost, pow'r divine, Cleanse this guilty heart of mine;
Long has sin without control Held dominion o'er my soul.

3. Holy Ghost, joy divine, Cheer this saddened heart of mine;
Bid my many woes depart, Heal my wounded, bleeding heart.

4. Holy Ghost, all divine, Dwell within this heart of mine;
Cast down ev'ry idol throne, Reign supreme and reign alone.

Respond

Are any sins controlling you, holding dominion over your soul, and keeping you from living a holy life?

_____

_____

_____

Do you have any idols that need to be cast off the throne of your life, so that the Holy Spirit may reign supreme?

_____

_____

_____

Prayer

Forgiving Savior, I repent, change my mind and purpose; I turn around and return to You that my sins may be erased, blotted out, wiped clean, that times of refreshing may come from You. I will cleanse myself from all filthiness of the flesh and spirit, perfecting holiness in fear and reverence of You, O God. I will throw off my old evil nature and my former way of life, which is rotten through and through, full of lust and deception. Instead, I will be spiritually renewed in my thoughts and attitudes. I will display a new nature because I am like a new person, created in Your likeness, Lord—righteous, holy, and true. (Acts 3:19 AMP; 2 Cor. 7:1b KJV; Eph. 4:22-24 NLT paraphrased)

Quiet Listening (15 to 30 minutes)

As you quiet your thoughts before the Lord, you will battle both outward and inward distractions. Keep persevering; keep bringing your thoughts back to God. Ask Him to help you hear Him and to overcome any thoughts that are not from Him. Then record your responses, confess sins and struggles, and note how the Lord has spiritually refreshed your thirst for holiness.

Respond

_____

_____

_____

Hymn to Sing or Reflect On

FILL ME NOW

1. Hover o'er me, Holy Spirit,
Bathe my trembling heart and brow;
Fill me with Thy hallowed presence,
Come, O come and fill me now.
Chorus:

Fill me now, fill me now,
Jesus, come and fill me now;
Fill me with Thy hallowed presence,
Come, O come and fill me now.

2. Thou canst fill me, gracious Spirit,
Though I cannot tell Thee how;
But I need Thee, greatly need Thee,
Come, O come and fill me now.

3. I am weakness, full of weakness,
At Thy sacred feet I bow;
Blest, divine, eternal Spirit,
Fill with power, and fill me now.

4. Cleanse and comfort, bless and save me,
Bathe, O bathe my heart and brow;
Thou art comforting and saving,
Thou art sweetly filling now.

Respond

In what situations or areas of your life do you need the Holy Spirit's cleansing, comfort, and power?

_____

_____

_____

_____

_____

_____

Recreation and Refreshment

Take a brief walk and have a light snack if you need to.

Scripture Reading: Revelation 21:1-7

Practicing the Spiritual Life

What does God promise the bride of Christ?

_____

_____

_____

What will the Alpha and Omega give those who are thirsty?

_____

_____

_____

_____

If Jesus asked you now to prepare yourself to be His bride, what would He ask you to do to get ready to meet Him?

_____

_____

_____

_____

Hymn to Sing or Reflect On

TAKE TIME TO BE HOLY

1. Take time to be holy, Speak oft with the Lord;
Abide in Him always, and feed on His word.
Make friends of God's children; Help those who are weak;
Forgetting in nothing His blessing to seek.

2. Take time to be holy, The world rushes on;
Much time spend in secret with Jesus alone;
By looking to Jesus, like Him you will be;
Your friends in your conduct His likeness shall see.

3. Take time to be holy, Let Him be your guide,
And run not before Him, whatever betide;
In joy or in sorrow still follow the Lord,
And looking to Jesus, still trust in His Word.

4. Take time to be holy, Be calm in your soul;
Each thought and each motive beneath His control;
Thus led by His Spirit to fountains of love,
You soon shall be fitted for service above.

Respond

In what ways are we to take time to be holy?

_____

_____

_____

How did this hymn speak to you about taking time to be holy?

_____

_____

_____

Prayer

As Your little child, Jesus, I will abide in You. I will lift up hands to Your Word, which I have loved; I will meditate and feed on Your Word. Now prepare me for works of service, so that Your body, Christ, may be built up. May the service that I perform not only supply the needs of God's people but also overflow in many expressions of thanks to You, O God. For I am looking to You, Jesus, the author and finisher of my faith. And I, with open face beholding as in a glass Your glory, Lord, am being changed into Your same image and likeness from glory to glory, even as by Your Spirit. (1 John 2:28a; Ps. 119:48 KJV; Eph. 4:12; 2 Cor. 9:12; Heb. 12:2a; 2 Cor. 3:18 KJV paraphrased)

Quiet Listening (15 to 30 minutes)

> *"Make every effort to live in peace with all men*
> *and to be holy; without holiness no one will see the Lord."*
>
> HEBREWS 12:14

Respond

_____

_____

_____

_____

MIDDAY

Refreshment, Recreation, and Rest (30 minutes to 1 hour)

Have lunch, walk, and rest. Relax and enjoy this break. Make it a time of praise, thanksgiving, and worship.

AFTERNOON QUIET TIME

Scripture Reading: Revelation 22:12-17

Practicing the Spiritual Life

What does the water of life cost those who are thirsty?

_____

_____

On what is our reward in heaven based?

_____

_____

If Jesus were to come to you now, what do you believe He might ask you to do to serve Him?

_____

_____

_____

_____

Hymn to Sing or Reflect On

HOLY, HOLY, HOLY

1. Holy, Holy, Holy! Lord God Almighty!
Early in the morning our song shall rise to Thee;
Holy, Holy, Holy! merciful and mighty!
God in three persons, blessed Trinity!

2. Holy, Holy, Holy! All the saints adore Thee,
Casting down their golden crowns around the glassy sea;
Cherubim and seraphim falling down before Thee,
Which wert and art and evermore shalt be.

3. Holy, Holy, Holy! Though the darkness hide Thee,
Though the eye of sinful man Thy glory may not see;
Only Thou art Holy—there is none beside Thee,
Perfect in pow'r, in love and purity.

4. Holy, Holy, Holy! Lord God Almighty!
All Thy works shall praise Thy name in earth and sky and sea;
Holy, Holy, Holy! merciful and mighty!
God in three persons, blessed Trinity!

Respond

As you reflect on the hymn, worship and praise the Lord. Write your own praises to the Lord God Almighty.

_____

_____

_____

Prayer

"'Holy, holy, holy is the Lord God Almighty, who was, and is, and is to come.'" Great are You, Lord, and most worthy of praise, in the city of my God, Your holy mountain. You are the Mighty One, O God, the Lord, who speaks and summons the earth from the rising of the sun to the place where it sets. Gracious are You, Lord, and righteous; yes, my God is merciful. My mouth will speak in praise of You, Lord. Let every creature praise Your holy name for ever and ever. (Rev. 4:8b not paraphrased; Ps. 48:1; 50:1; Ps. 116:5 KJV; Ps. 145:21 paraphrased)

Quiet Listening (15 to 30 minutes)

"O Lord God Almighty, who is like you?
You are mighty, O Lord,
and your faithfulness surrounds you."

PSALM 89:8

Respond

Recreation and Refreshment

Take a brief walk and have a light snack if you need to.

Review and Respond

Read over what you've written in your responses. Has the Lord guided you in a special way through the Scriptures, hymns, retreat setting, or during your prayers and quiet listening? If so, what do you feel the Lord has impressed on your heart and mind?

How has the Lord ministered to you and satisfied your spiritual thirst?

Are there any commitments that you would like to make to the Lord? If so, set a specific time period to fulfill the commitments.

In the days ahead, what do you desire the Lord to do for you as you seek to lead a more holy life?

_____

_____

_____

BLESSED QUIETNESS

1. Joys are flowing like a river,
Since the Comforter has come;
He abides with us forever,
Makes the trusting heart His home.
Chorus:

Blessed quietness, holy quietness,
What assurance in my soul!
On the stormy sea He speaks peace to me,
How the billows cease to roll!

3. Like the rain that falls from heaven,
Like the sunlight from the sky,
So the Holy Ghost is given,
Coming on us from on high.

5. What a wonderful salvation,
Where we always see His face!
What a perfect habitation,
What a quiet resting place!

APPENDIX:

Plans for a Small Group Study and Spiritual Retreat

Although *A Woman's Journey Toward Holiness* was written for individuals, it can also be used by groups. The twelve weeks of devotional studies make it ideal for a quarterly class schedule. The thirteenth week is a spiritual retreat that you will need to plan for and schedule.

You may find that holding the class for an hour is too brief. Ninety minutes for the study and light refreshments is ideal. This creates an informal atmosphere and allows for more personal sharing and prayer time.

A home may be more comfortable than a classroom for this kind of devotional study. But if you meet in a classroom and the setting is less than ideal, you can still set the right tone. Our class met in the preschoolers' room of our church. Every week, I put the toys away and set up a portable screen to block off part of the play area. I decorated a small table with either a crocheted or lace cloth, lighted candles, flowers, or other simple decorations that correlated with the theme of the study.

A week before the first meeting, make sure the members of the class have this book. Ask them to read and do the devotionals for Week One, "Respond to Christ's Call to Be Holy." Then you will be able to begin group discussion right away.

Leader Preparation

Plan to cover the weekly chapters in one or two class sessions. You'll have enough time to cover the introductory material and seven devotionals if you take two sessions, extending the class to twenty-four weeks. If you choose to cover the entire chapter and devotionals during one class session, decide which statements or questions from "Practicing the Spiritual Life" you will use for discussion.

As you read over the chapter and do the devotions each week, highlight or underline the main points and spiritual applications. Note the ways the Lord ministers to you as you read the chapter and do the devotions. Then share with the class personal examples of how the Lord spoke to your heart and helped you.

The more committed you are to leading a holy life, the more you will encourage others in the group to do the same. At the same time, be transparent about your own spiritual struggles. If you present yourself as the perfect Christian, class members will be discouraged about their own weaknesses.

Prayer is an essential part of your preparation. Pray for class members, and let them know you are doing so. Pray that they will grow in Christ and be strengthened in their faith and commitment to become more godly. Pray for the class sessions that the Lord will have His hand on them and lead you in guiding the discussion. Pray for the Holy Spirit's guidance and wisdom. Pray that your own desire for holiness will increase.

Small Group Guidelines

Though some women may not feel comfortable writing in a published book, encourage them to do so. They may also want to use notebook paper or a journal to write additional comments, verses, or spiritual insights.

Have the women sit in a circle, semicircle, or around a table. This makes the class more personal and facilitates discussion. Women who are hard of hearing try to read lips and facial expressions, so they especially need to see the persons speaking.

If the class is large, divide it into groups of four to eight women. Either choose discussion leaders, or ask the groups to choose their own. Many women feel more comfortable sharing when there are fewer members. This also allows them to participate more, and they can get to know each other in a more personal way.

Encourage the women to read the chapter and complete the devotionals prior to each session. Lack of preparation limits the discussion, because fewer women are ready to share, and lessens the benefits for those who did not prepare.

Encourage the women to underline and reflect on passages in the text that were especially meaningful to them. Ask them to return to class ready to share spiritual insights and/or questions. This will make the class more interesting and will be an incentive for the other members.

Class Session Plans

Set a devotional atmosphere. I played Christian music cassettes softly as members arrived. We spent the first five minutes quietly listening to hymns and worship songs. This provided a peaceful setting that helped the women release their tensions and gave them an opportunity to pray, worship, and spiritually prepare themselves.

The weekly title page has a Scripture passage that the women may use for memorization. Memorizing is difficult for some women, so be careful not to embarrass those who don't learn the verses. Other women may want to memorize some of the verses but not all of them.

This devotional study is for women in different stages of spiritual growth. Encourage those who may feel embarrassed because they don't have devotions or who feel guilty about the amount of time they spend with the Lord. Others may try to have devotions but can't keep their thoughts focused, or they may come away feeling dry or dissatisfied. This class is for all seekers who desire to lead a holy life.

Here is a format that you might follow for the class:

Open with prayer and a hymn or worship songs that correlate with the theme of the study. If you don't have someone who can play the piano or guitar, use cassette tapes you can sing along with, or sing without an instrument.

If you have one small group, discuss together the highlights of the chapter and the questions or statements from "Practicing the Spiritual Life." If the class is large, you might briefly share highlights from the introductory material, giving personal illustrations from your own spiritual journey. Then the class can go to their small groups to discuss the devotionals.

Close in prayer, asking women to share prayer requests briefly. Encourage the group to pray for each other during the week. They may write prayer requests in their books under "Prayers, Praises, and Personal Notes."

If time permits, have light refreshments after the session. This will allow the women time to share informally. This will also give them the opportunity to ask you questions that they didn't feel comfortable discussing with the group. They may need to share personal concerns or burdens with you. If you have group leaders, ask them to be available to the women in their groups during this time.

Most women are busy and work long hours, so it is important to begin and end on time as much as possible. Those who want to stay for refreshments will, and those who need to leave will do so.

Group Discussion Guidelines

Open discussion and group participation are the best methods for using this devotional material. Women remember more of what they do and say, so keep lectures to a minimum. Be a facilitator who guides the discussion and keeps the class on track and on schedule.

Be relaxed, and the class will feel more at ease. This doesn't mean that the class is unstructured. Maintain an informal friendly manner while guiding the discussion in an orderly way.

Involve as many women as possible. You might go around the group, asking each member to answer different questions or contribute a comment. Women who don't feel comfortable entering into the discussion may be willing to read Scripture aloud.

Ask the group to share personal examples of what they learned in the devotional study or of how God has been working in their lives and changing them. The more the women see that the Lord can change their lives and others, the more enthusiastic they may be about growing in their faith and leading a holy life.

Some women may feel uncomfortable answering the personal questions about their spiritual life. Others will gladly volunteer. Respect their comfort level.

The group will gain more from the class if you keep the discussion on track. If the women get off onto tangents, bring the discussion back to the main topic as quickly as possible.

Keep more vocal members from dominating the group. When a person keeps talking without pausing, you may have to interrupt. You might say something like this, "Excuse me, we appreciate what you have to say, but we need to give others an opportunity to share." Then ask another person to contribute an answer.

Everyone is in a different place spiritually. Some of the women will be mature; others will be new believers. Some will be committed to growing in their faith; others will have little desire at all. Some women have been Christians for many years but have not grown in their faith. They may be defensive, embarrassed, or unaware of their spiritual condition. Still others may be angry, bitter, and/or rebellious due to a painful church experience.

Most of us feel inferior around people who seem to have all the correct answers and can quote the right verse for every difficulty. Such people may also spiritualize their problems and appear to handle their lives in a perfect manner, no matter how many trials they face. Others around them may feel that they are being judged or that they do not measure up to the standards of perfect Christians.

Set an open, accepting tone by constantly affirming those who may feel that they aren't as spiritual. Be gracious and kind to those who are hurting deeply and/or questioning their faith. Be patient and loving with those who may have bitter attitudes. Pray for the transforming power of the Holy Spirit to work in all of your lives.

We all need the assurance that our Lord loves us with a love that is beyond our comprehension. Because He loves us so much, He will always be available to support and strengthen us as we grow in Him, and we need to do the same for each other.

The Spiritual Retreat

A retreat for spiritual renewal may also be called a silent retreat, because the women will be spending time alone with the Lord without talking to each other. During this time they will be using the Week Thirteen, "Refresh Your Thirst for Holiness," spiritual retreat guide and their Bibles.

Silence is maintained until the early afternoon when the group gathers for sharing, worship, Communion, and fellowship. Though the idea of being with others without speaking may seem difficult, the group will discover that this time alone with the Lord will be spiritually renewing.

When I first mentioned to my class that we would be spending a morning together without talking, they couldn't imagine that it would be possible. At the end of the retreat, however, they felt that the time had gone by too quickly and were already talking about having another one.

The women will need reassurance, because they will feel uncomfortable about not speaking to the others. A silent devotional retreat has an added dimension that you may miss when you have a retreat alone. You feel the prayers and the presence of Lord when many are gathered together. You feel spiritually strengthened and uplifted by the other women even though you aren't talking with them.

Group Retreat Plans

Choose a quiet, peaceful place for the retreat. We had a one-day retreat at a home with a lovely garden and pool. A small park was a block away. Some women sat by the pool, others in the front yard, while others went to the park. If you have a conference center nearby, you may be able to use their grounds for a day.

Set a day and time for the retreat. We had ours on a Saturday from 9:30 A.M. to 3:30 P.M. Depending on the desires of your group, you may want to start earlier and/or go later in the day.

Make a sign-up sheet for the women to help with setup and cleanup and to bring food and paper goods. Keep food simple and light; we had sandwiches for lunch. We also had coffee, juice, sodas, muffins, and fresh fruit available throughout the day for snacks. For our afternoon fellowship time we had a light dessert.

We didn't have the morning snack or lunch together. Some women set up the snack while others laid out the food for lunch. Others took care of cleaning up. We maintained our time of silence during this time and until we met for worship and fellowship in the afternoon.

Have a closing worship and Communion service and a fellowship time with a snack. Sing hymns and worship songs during the worship time. Ask the women to share how the Lord ministered to them during the retreat. Then close with Communion.

The retreat guide, "Refresh Your Thirst for Holiness," would also work well for a weekend retreat. I have been on a private spiritual retreat at a center where we remained silent until the evening meal. At that time, we shared around the table and had an evening worship and prayer service. Sunday morning could include a time of silence followed by a worship service and Communion.

Our retreat was a spiritually renewing experience. For me, it was life-changing as I sat at Jesus' feet and felt His powerful presence in the love and prayers of my friends. The Lord sent me out from that time with a greater desire to serve Him.

It is my prayer, that as you go forth to comfort, minister, and serve others, you may be filled with joyous praise as you watch with wonder the transforming work of the Lord in your life and the lives of others.

NOTES

WEEK ONE: RESPOND TO CHRIST'S CALL TO BE HOLY

1. R. C. Sproul, *The Holiness of God* (Wheaton, Ill.: Tyndale House Publishers, Inc., 1985), 61.
2. Ibid., 65.
3. Jerry Bridges, *The Pursuit of Holiness* (Colorado Springs: Navpress, 1978), 19.
4. *The Confession of Faith*, modern language (Edinburgh: University Press, 1855), 222-24.
5. Bridges, *Pursuit*, 40-41.
6. *Confession of Faith*, 208.

WEEK TWO: RECEIVE GOD'S GRACE

1. "Hands Across the Water," *In Focus*, vol. 1, no. 2, Wycliffe Bible Translators, April/May 1996. [No page number or author.]
2. Charles R. Swindoll, *The Grace Awakening* (Dallas: Word Publishing, 1990), 201.
3. Dietrich Bonhoeffer, *The Cost of Discipleship* (New York: Macmillan Publishing Co., Inc., 1959), 46.
4. Ibid., 47-48.
5. Swindoll, *Grace Awakening*, 202.

WEEK THREE: RESOLVE TO WIN THE WAR FOR HOLINESS

1. Alexander G. Higgins, "Pinpointing Bosnia's Passive Killers," *Santa Maria Times*, 27 May 1996, sec. A.
2. Wm. J. Castello, "Land Mines," *Santa Maria Times*, 27 May 1996, sec. A.
3. Higgins, "Pinpointing Killers."
4. Jerry Bridges, *The Pursuit of Holiness* (Colorado Springs: Navpress, 1978), 60.
5. Ibid., 69.
6. Ibid., 84.
7. Ibid., 20-21.
8. Gordon MacDonald, *Rebuilding Your Broken World* (Nashville: Oliver Nelson, 1988), xiv.
9. Bridges, *Pursuit*, 21.
10. MacDonald, *Rebuilding*, 22-23.
11. Bridges, *Pursuit*, 87.
12. Ibid., 66.
13. Ibid., 83.
14. Ibid., 71.

WEEK FOUR: REVERE GOD'S HOLY ATTRIBUTES

1. John K. Ryan, trans., *The Confessions of St. Augustine* (New York: Image, Doubleday, 1960), 43.

2. *The Confession of Faith* (Edinburgh: University Press, 1855), 29-31.

3. A. W. Tozer, *The Knowledge of the Holy* (San Francisco: HarperSan Francisco, 1961), 78-79.

4. Ibid., 78-79.

5. Ibid., 79.

6. Ibid., 98.

7. J. I. Packer, *Knowing God* (Downers Grove, Ill.: InterVarsity Press, 1973), 86.

8. Tozer, *Knowledge of the Holy,* 105-06.

9. William Evans, *The Great Doctrines of the Bible* (Chicago: Moody Press, 1912), 40.

10. Tozer, *Knowledge of the Holy,* 107.

11. Ibid., viii.

12. Ibid., 49.

13. Ibid., 51-52.

14. Ibid., 91-92.

15. Ibid., 81.

16. Ibid., 39.

WEEK FIVE: RECOGNIZE LIFE'S UNCERTAINTIES

1. Oswald Chambers, *My Utmost for His Highest* (New York: Dodd, Mead & Company, Inc., 1935), October 30, 304.

2. Judie Frank, "Take Them Back," copyright 1996. All rights reserved. Used by permission.

WEEK SIX: RELINQUISH YOUR HEART'S DESIRES

1. Oswald Chambers, *My Utmost for His Highest* (New York: Dodd, Mead & Company, Inc., 1935), June 4, 156.

2. Ibid., June 5, 157.

3. Catherine Marshall, *Beyond Ourselves* (New York: McGraw-Hill Book Company, Inc., 1961), 87.

4. Ibid., 94.

5. Ibid., 88.

6. Larry Crabb, *Inside Out* (Colorado Springs: Navpress, 1988), 18.

7. Chambers, *My Utmost,* April 4, 95.

8. Marshall, *Beyond Ourselves,* 86.

9. Ibid., 86.

10. Ibid., 94.

WEEK SEVEN: RELEASE YOUR LIFE TO GOD

1. Corrie ten Boom, Jamie Buckingham, *Tramp for the Lord* (Old Tappan, N.J.: Fleming H. Revell Company, 1974), 11.

2. Ibid., 12.

3. Ibid., 152-53.

4. Corrie ten Boom, *A Tramp Finds a Home* (Old Tappan, N.J.: Fleming H. Revell Company, 1978), 7.

5. ten Boom, Buckingham, *Tramp for the Lord*, 44.
6. Ibid., 45.
7. Ibid., 33.
8. Ibid., 185-86.
9. Oswald Chambers, *My Utmost for His Highest* (New York: Dodd, Mead & Company, Inc., 1935), June 15, 167.
10. ten Boom, Buckingham, *Tramp for the Lord*, 78.

WEEK EIGHT: REALIZE THE NEED TO CHANGE

1. Corrie ten Boom, Jamie Buckingham, *Tramp for the Lord* (Old Tappan, N.J.: Fleming H. Revell Company, 1974), 60.
2. Ibid., 181.
3. J. I. Packer, *Knowing God* (Downers Grove, Ill.: InterVarsity Press, 1973), 117.
4. Larry Crabb, *Inside Out* (Colorado Springs: Navpress, 1988), 33-34.
5. Ibid., 34.
6. Hannah Whitall Smith, *The Christian's Secret of a Happy Life* (Old Tappan, N.J.: Fleming H. Revell Company, 1952), 53-4.
7. Ibid.
8. Charles R. Swindoll, *The Grace Awakening* (Dallas: Word Publishing, 1990), 19.
9. Melvin E. Dieter, Anthony A. Hoekema, et al., *Five Views of Sanctification* (Grand Rapids: Zondervan Publishing House, 1987), 29.
10. Ibid., 66.
11. Ibid., 64.
12. Ibid., 67.

WEEK NINE: RELY ON GOD'S GUIDANCE

1. M. Blaine Smith, *Knowing God's Will: Biblical Principles of Guidance* (Downers Grove, Ill.: InterVarsity Press, 1969), 17-18.
2. Ibid., 18.
3. Elisabeth Elliot, *A Slow and Certain Light: Some Thoughts on the Guidance of God* (Waco: Word Books, Publishers, 1973), 29.
4. Oswald Chambers, *My Utmost for His Highest* (New York: Dodd, Mead & Company, Inc., 1935), May 15, 136.
5. Elliot, *Slow and Certain Light*, 49.
6. Ibid.
7. Roy and Revel Hession, *We Would See Jesus* (Fort Washington, Penn.: Christian Literature Crusade, 1958), 70.
8. Elliot, *Slow and Certain Light*, 38.
9. Ibid., 40.
10. Hession, *We Would See Jesus*, 70.
11. J. I. Packer, *Knowing God* (Downers Grove, Ill.: InterVarsity Press, 1973), 212.
12. Throughout Scripture men and women were led by supernatural guidance, fleeces, prophecies, and visions. The subject of supernatural guidance requires greater coverage

than can be addressed in this brief chapter. For more information on supernatural guidance, see Elisabeth Elliot's book, *A Slow and Certain Light: Some Thoughts on the Guidance of God.*

13. Ibid., 87-91.
14. Ibid., 103-08.

WEEK TEN: RUN A DISCIPLINED RACE

1. Jerry Bridges, *The Pursuit of Holiness* (Colorado Springs: Navpress, 1978), 98.
2. Henri J. M. Nouwen, *Making All Things New: An Invitation to the Spiritual Life* (San Francisco: Harper & Row, Publishers, 1981), 45-46.
3. Ibid., 46-47.
4. Ibid., 47-49.
5. Bill Gasser, "The Run," *The Baptist Bulletin,* October 1996, 10-11.
6. Oswald Chambers, *My Utmost for His Highest* (New York: Dodd, Mead & Company, Inc., 1935), October 12, 286.
7. Bridges, *Pursuit of Holiness,* 101.
8. Ibid., 102.
9. Gasser, "The Run," 11.
10. Ibid.
11. Bridges, *Pursuit of Holiness,* 106.
12. Gasser, "The Run," 11.

WEEK ELEVEN: REMEMBER TO GIVE THE GIFT OF GRACE

1. Charles R. Swindoll, *The Grace Awakening* (Dallas: Word Publishing, 1990), 208.

WEEK TWELVE: REJOICE IN THE LORD ALWAYS

1. Jack Hayford, *The Heart of Praise: Daily Ways to Worship the Father with Psalms* (Ventura: Regal Books, 1992), 22.
2. A. W. Tozer, *The Knowledge of the Holy* (San Francisco: HarperSan Francisco, 1961), 106.
3. Hayford, *Heart of Praise,* 22-23.
4. Tozer, *Knowledge of the Holy,* 114.
5. Ibid., 115.
6. Charles Spurgeon, *Psalms,* The Crossway Classic Commentaries, Vol. 1, ed. Alister McGrath, J. I. Packer (Wheaton, Ill.: Crossway Books, 1993), 127.
7. Tozer, *Knowledge of the Holy,* 108.
8. *The Confession of Faith* (Edinburgh: University Press, 1855), 106-08.
9. Spurgeon, *Psalms,* 207-08.
10. Ibid., 304.
11. Ibid., 25.
12. Ibid., 303-04.

INDEX

splendor of, 26
standing in holy presence of, 190-91
trustworthy, 24
unchanging, 61, 63-64, 70
unseen hand of, 92-93
wisdom of, 41, 60, 152
Godliness
definition of, 16
grow in, 19
pursue, 22
Godly Life, See Holy Life
God's Word, See Word of God
Good
deeds, 36, 40, 185
doing, 36, 185
love of, 22
seek, 119
work, 69
Goodness, fruit of the Spirit, 128
Gospel, 119
Grace
cheap, 32-33
compassionate, 175-76
costly, 32-34
demonstrate, 39
for weakness, 33-34
gifts of, 174-75, 186
giving, 179
heavenly, 34
humble, 176-77
increased, 32
perfected in weakness, 33
riches of, 49
sacrificial gifts of, 175, 177-79
sanctifying, 30-32
saved by, 29, 32-33
sufficiency of, 33
under, 38
versus works, 29, 32-33
Greed, 35, 51, 154
Grief, 95-96, 98, 100, 128-29
Guidance
conditions for receiving, 142-44

for benefit of others, 143-44
God's, 83
Jesus as the Way to, 144-45
means of, 145-47
moral decisions, 140-47
obtaining, 152
personal decisions, 141-47
Guilt, 32, 38

Heart
broken, 98
changed, 112-13
deceitful, 45
desires of, 97
encourage, 40
fill with joy, 195
fill with peace, 195
humble, 196
in God's hand, 150
law within, 115
loyalty of, 195
pure, 23, 25, 57, 63
search, 101
seeks God, 200
sincere, 55
tested, 136
undivided, 148
Heaven/s
beholding face of God in, 19
citizens of, 31, 34
eternal home, 66
former things not remembered, 34
God set in place, 120
made perfect in holiness in, 19
new, 34
Help, from God, 93, 100
Holiness
battle for, 34
beauty of Christ's, 191
call to, 32, 177
definition of, 16, 31
fear of, 16-17
journey toward, 109